20 Herbs for Your Wedding

Avia Lukacs &
Therese Francis

Herb & Spice Pantry
an imprint of the Crossquarter Publishing Group
PO Box 23749
Santa Fe, NM 87502

ISBN Paperback: 978-1-890109-01-1
Hardcover ISBN: 978-1-890109-02-8
e-Book ISBN: 978-1-890109-03-5

Disclaimer: The herbs and foods in this book are based on the
authors' experience and are not intended to diagnose, treat, or
prevent illness or disease. Furthermore, all herbs, flowers and foods
are potential allergens. The authors do not accept responsibility
regarding an individual's response to anything mentioned or
implied in this book.

Library of Congress Cataloging-in-Publication Data

Names: Lukacs, Avia, 1957- author | Francis, Therese, author.
Title: 20 herbs for your wedding / Avia Lukacs & Therese Francis.
Other titles: Twenty herbs for your wedding
Description: Santa Fe, NM : Herb & Spice Pantry, [2015] | Includes
  bibliographical references and index. | Description based on print
  version record and CIP data provided by publisher; resource not viewed.
Identifiers: LCCN 2015046851 (print) | LCCN 2015046514 (ebook) |
  ISBN 9781890109035 () | ISBN 9781890109011 (pbk. : alk. paper)
Subjects: LCSH: Herbs--Utilization. | Wedding decorations.
Classification: LCC SB449.5.W4 (print) | LCC SB449.5.W4 L84 2015
  (ebook) | DDC 635/.7--dc23
LC record available at http://lccn.loc.gov/2015046851

Other Books by the Authors

20 Herbs on Your Honeymoon

20 Herbs to Take Outdoors:
  an herbal first aid primer for the outdoor enthusiast

20 Herbs in My Broom Closet:
  green cleaning

20 Herbs in My Coffee Cup:
  herbal replacement for that morning pick-me-up

20 Herbs for Counting Sheep:
  herbal ideas to help you relax and sleep

Table of Contents

Overview

The first section of this book introduces the most historically common herbs that are included in weddings and wedding preparations. Many of them you have heard of but may not have realized they could hold a place on your special day.

The second section gives ideas and instructions for different parts of your wedding from unique invitations to center pieces for the reception tables.

The third section is how these herbs can be used to pamper you and your wedding party.

And finally the food section with lots of recipes for everything from beverages for the engagement party to formal wedding feasts. *Bon appétit.*

Abbreviations used throughout:

C = cup(s)
Tbsp = tablespoon(s)
tsp = teaspoon(s)
lb/lbs = pound(s)
Qt = quart(s)
oz. = ounce

All temperatures are in degrees Fahrenheit.

Section 1:
Introducing the
Herbal Wedding Party

This first section is an introduction to the herbs that have been used in weddings throughout the world. Each herb has a bit about growing it (if you so desire), some history, and fun trivia.

Angelica

(Angelica archangelica)

Angelica is a tall plant that can get as high as eight feet, therefore, it makes a good plant to provide privacy or fencing. The stalk is round, purplish and divides into many branches with each branch holding many flower clusters. The flowers are white or greenish in color and are very sweet smelling. Angelica is easy to start from seeds, as are most herbs; they tend to be strong, hearty and as easy to grow as weeds. Angelica is a biennial which means it will come up every other year, so leave room when planting in the ground to allow the plant to re-seed itself and propagate for the next year. This plant likes moist soil and does not need full sun. In the wild, it looks like its poisonous cousin, water hemlock, so we don't recommend wild crafting this plant.

Angelica is the angel plant. It is affiliated with the divine and named after Michael the Archangel whom is the patron saint against temptations and the protector of children. Historically, the plant itself was believed to have heavenly powers of protection – much like Michael; hence, the namesake.

Peasants would make necklaces by braiding the stems together. They then put the necklaces on their children believing it would ward off evil spirits.

These necklaces were also worn in matrimony rituals, spring festivals and other celebrations. Since angelica traditionally was found at a wedding, see Section 4 for a recipe that uses angelica on the wedding cake.

Herbs historically have been used for their medicinal properties. In medieval times, angelica tea was thought a cure for the plague. Today, angelica is used to alleviate bronchial infections and aide in digestion. It is known to be a good tonic for the heart, circulation and female ailments. Angelica is used in aromatherapy in skin care for psoriasis, for muscle and joint pain for arthritis and rheumatism, and to ease respiratory problems and coughs, and as an aide to indigestion. The cosmetic industry uses angelica in soaps, lotions and perfumes.

Angelica is used in many foods and beverages. The stems can be steamed and eaten like asparagus or crystallized and eaten as candy. Fresh leaves can be used in salads and soups but go light as fresh leaves have a strong flavor much like juniper. Dried leaves are added to breads, muffins, cakes and cookies. Stems, roots, seeds and leaves are all used in teas, tonics and herbal liqueurs – most popular in flavoring of gin and vermouth. Candied angelica stems can be used to decorate the wedding cake or served as a confection.

Basil

(Ocimum basilicum)

Basil is a 1-2 foot high bushy plant. It is a tender annual that grows easily from seed. The plant likes well-drained rich soil and full sunlight. Basil planted next to peppers and tomatoes is said to encourage their growth. It does not like cold weather and works well in a pot that can be carried indoors during winter months.

Basil is originally from India. It has many varieties. One way to determine the variety is by the smell. The table below indicates a few of the more popular varieties.

Variety	Flower Color	Fragrance
Lemon	White	Lemon
Anise	White	Anise or Licorice
Cinnamon	White	Cinnamon
Thyrsiflora	White & Deep Lavender	Sweet
Clove	White with Yellow Anthers	Clove
Camphor	White with Red Anthers	Camphor or Menthol

Basil is the herb that symbolizes love. According to Italian tradition if a woman placed a pot of basil outside of her window she was indicating that she was ready for her lover. In Moldavia, if a man gives a woman a sprig of fresh basil that woman will fall helplessly in love with him and never leave him. It was considered a sacred herb to the Hindu Gods Krishna and Vishnu.

Basil is best known for its culinary uses. Since basil is so easy to grow, it is readily available fresh, so use fresh when you can. Basil leaves can be used to flavor eggs, cheese, soups, fish, vegetables, salads, poultry, red meats and breads.

Did you know?
Pesto is considered a love dish or aphrodisiac.

Bay Laurel

(Laurus nobilis)

Bay is an evergreen tree with glossy green leaves, olive green or red bark, with small white flowers. This perennial is easily grown in containers but in colder climates it does need to be brought in during the winter months. Grow in a sheltered sunny position with well-drained soil and prune regularly. It is a native of the Mediterranean region. It is also called laurel and sweet bay.

Bay laurel leaves can be air dried in about two weeks and then stored in airtight containers. *Laurus nobilis* is the only type of laurel that can be used in cooking and most everyone can recognize it easily by its full rounded green leaf.

Bay is best known for its flavoring and used most often in stews and soups.

Bay is strongly antiseptic and aromatic, and therefore used as a fragrance component in detergents, cosmetics, toiletries and perfumes. Oil from leaf and berries are used to treat bruises and rheumatism. In ancient times it was believed to promote menstruation. It has narcotic properties and the oil should not be ingested.

Historically, bay is a symbol of glory, reward and achievement. The leaves were woven into laurel wreaths to crown the victors of ancient Greek and Roman Olympics, political leaders, kings, priests, Gods and Goddesses. Apollo, the Greek God of the sun, was in love with Daphne who wanted nothing to do with him. Daphne's indifference was really the result of Cupid's arrow that made her hate him. Apollo was unaware that Cupid's arrow had turned Daphne away from him and he chased her endlessly. Daphne's father, Peneus changed her into a laurel tree so that she could escape Apollo. Apollo fell on his knees before the laurel tree and declared his eternal love for her and mandated that the tree be deemed sacred. From then on he wore a laurel wreath upon his head in symbol of his eternal love for Daphne.

Did you know?
Bay laurel wreaths were given to Olympian winners.

Caraway

(Carum carvi)

The caraway plant, a biennial herb, seeds itself every two years. Therefore, plan accordingly if you want continual harvesting. Plant the seeds ¼" deep and about an inch apart in full sun. They like sandy soil with good drainage. In cooler climates bring in during winter months. When thinning keep the strongest plants about a foot apart as they will get bushy growing up to two feet high and a foot wide.

Hearty and easy to grow, caraway is easily recognized by the divided leaves and full clusters of white flowers. Caraway is native to Europe and parts of Asia, India and North Africa.

Caraway is used medicinally for stomach ailments. In Shakespeare's "Henry IV" the character Falstaff is offered a plate of baked apples with caraway to aide digestion and relieve gas. Current alternative therapies suggest tea of caraway mixed with peppermint to alleviate irritable bowel syndrome.

Did you know?
Caraway seeds can insure fidelity.

Caraway historically was thought to have preventative spiritual properties and was used in many love potions. It was believed that by placing caraway in an object it would prevent theft of that object. Thus, if you placed seeds in your lover's pockets it would prevent your lover's love from being stolen away from you or straying.

Although they are popularly referred to as "seeds" caraway technically is a fruit, and is generally used in cooking dried (not fresh). A very popular herb, it smells and tastes somewhat like licorice. Chewing the seeds will act as a breath freshener and reduce gas. Little finger bowls filled with a mix of caraway, cardamom, mint and parsley sprigs placed on the wedding dinner table will be appreciated by guests.

Caraway seeds are used worldwide. The English make cake out of it; Hungarians use it in their stews; Germans in their meats and the Swedish in their breads. Rye bread, sauerkraut and Havarti cheese are all flavored with caraway seeds.

Chickweed

(Stellaria media)

It is prolific and makes a good ground cover because stems are weak and rambling. This hearty weed is found almost everywhere throughout the world. The stems have little hairs on them that cover the new bud stems at night. The leaves are oval and small and sit in pairs with small white flowers. They bloom from spring until fall and grows year round even through cool damp weather.

Chickweed is one member of a large family of annual weeds that grow native to Europe and Asia. Chickweed is used as feed on some farms and is currently cultivated as fill in bird seed.

Chickweed is great in soups and salads and can be eaten alone as greens. Cooked greens are a lot like cooked spinach. The greens and the flowers can both be eaten in the salad.

Chickweed is very high in iron and is said to make a good tea for any and all female ailments as it has a balancing effect on the hormones. It is also noted as a natural laxative and an aide to digestion. Folklore has that it can cure obesity, but unfortunately that hasn't been proven.

Did you know?
Chickweed can reduce weight.

Chickweed is known to reduce the negative effects of alcohol and acts as a tonic to the liver. A chickweed salad the night before just might help reduce the hangover of too much partying.

Chickweed salads can be used in a wedding menu or would be great for an engagement party served with wine, a variety of sliced breads, a cheese plate, olives, stuffed mushrooms, scallops wrapped in bacon or any other appetizers.

Cowslip

(Primula veris)

These perennial flowers come in many colors and many variations. They prefer moist rich soil and do best in a partially shady area although in coastal regions they will tolerate full sun due to the additional moisture in the air. All varieties bloom early spring.

The cowslip is one member of a large family – a large family of flowers. The English primrose, oxlip and chickweed are more commonly known members.

Today, the cowslip is most enjoyed as an ornamental. The English primrose is the most popular. The juice from the flowers is thought to ease wrinkles when made into a tea and used as toner. Cowslip tea and wine are very popular. Evening primrose tea and the oil is used to ease the symptoms of PMS and menopause in women. The flower is edible as are the greens and are eaten alone or used in salads and desserts.

Did you know?
Cowslips are the keys to heaven.

The cowslip is also called the keyflower or Our Lady's Keys referring to the Virgin Mary. The flowers somewhat resemble a set of keys on the stalk. And in medieval times they were thought to be the keys to heaven. Historically, the wedding party all dressed alike in order to confuse any demons that might be trying to steal the bride. In Victorian times the bride maids even dressed in white with little veils. This was in an attempt to deceive any evil spirits from the true wedding couple.

Elderberry

(Sambucus)

Elder consists of thirteen species of shrubs growing from 12 ft to more treelike species growing to 50 ft. One of the easiest ways to propagate is from suckers (or trendil like outgrowths or crawly stems with little root nodules on them much like a raspberry bush). Cuttings or seeds can also be used. Elder is very hardy and does not require much attention, liking moist soil, full sun to partial shade. The elder will grow well under those conditions and the greatest chore may be controlling the suckers and new growth.

The elderberry has large creamy white wheel shaped clusters of flowers blooming in early summer. In the fall the elder produce berries of amber, red, black, purple or blue in color. The elder is native to North America and Europe and grows wild in both areas.

The elderberry has been used a fruit or in pies, jams, jellies, chutneys, juices and wine. The blossoms can be used in wines and tea blends with some medicinal effect and for centuries was considered the plant for healing all body ailments. To harvest the flowers pick when in full blooms. Blossoms can be used fresh, pickled by addition of about 10% common salt or allowed to air dry.

Did you know?
Elder branches are poisonous.

The amateur herbalist should embrace this plant carefully though as the leaves, stems and roots can be very dangerous. They contain substances that release cyanide and other poisons. Historically, in the seventeenth century young boys used the branches as play toys. The hollow branch was used as a blowgun or whistle. That is how they discovered the toxic nature as the young boys became sick from holding the elderberry branches in their mouths. In Denmark, the tradition holds that there is a spirit living in the elder and anyone that cuts one down will be haunted forever. On a lighter note, elder flower water was used by young ladies as lotion to lighten freckles and in bath water to soften the skin and relax nerves.

Fennel

(Foeniculum vulgare)

Fennel, a perennial that looks like dill, grows to a height of 5-6 ft. with feathery leaves and bright yellow flowers. It prefers a humus rich, well-drained soil and full sun. Care should be taken not to over water, but other than that it is fairly easy to grow for years as it self-seeds.

In medieval times, fennel was one of the nine sacred herbs with the power to cure the nine causes of medieval diseases and to ward off evil spirits. It was found in most herb gardens.

Most gardens were large with small areas within to sit privately for bathing, reading or meditation. These formal gardens usually had a central tree, often bay, hawthorn, a fruit or nut tree. Bushes would act as fences to protect the outside of the garden; commons ones were elderberry, raspberry, or huckleberry, or sometimes a trellis holding grapes. Inside the garden various herbs were matched in size and kind and planted in intricate geometric designs.

The "knot gardens" could be any size and some were designed as a maze to walk through with gravel paths. Knot gardens were the most popular with the English, French, and Celtics. Although they were quite popular in the past there are only a handful today available to tour. Fennel was a favorite in these gardens as it is sweetly aromatic in both odor and taste and for its detoxifying and relaxing properties.

When the fennel seeds turn from yellowish green to brown they are ready to be harvested. With scissors, simply cut the entire head off and store in a warm, dark place to dry. As with drying of any leaves, once dried they can be stored in airtight containers for a long time.

Did you know?
Fennel is a detoxifier.

Medicinal uses include curing colic in babies, relieving the swollen breasts of nursing mothers, expelling worms and as a breath freshener. As a tea it is used to cleanse impurities from the body and used as a detoxifier. It is considered a good liver tonic.

Hawthorn

(Crataegus oxyacanthas)

Hawthorn is hardy, grows well in any soil and tolerates either sun or partial shade. The hawthorn branches have thorns with small white or pink flowers. The seeds or berries on the tree are small and green when unripe and when ripened they fall to the ground as red berries.

The hawthorn tree is a member of the rose family. It is native to the Mediterranean, North Africa, Europe and Central Asia. It was originally the most popular in England and is now popular in America, where it is used as a hedge or natural fencing.

The wood of the hawthorn is a fine grain and is used by many artists in creating wooden boxes and combs.

The hawthorn has many medicinal and culinary uses. The berry is used as a cardiac tonic; a tea to treat high blood pressure and the leaves as a tobacco substitute. The hawthorn leaf buds when cooked taste similar to lima beans and are served in salads. Hawthorne berries contain their own pectin so sauce or jelly thickens naturally. Hawthorn is said to taste similar to coffee and is a decaffeinated substitute. Flowers are edible and can be added to salads or to decorate desserts, pies and cakes.

Did you know?
The hawthorn symbolizes marriage.

In ancient Greece and Rome, the hawthorn was associated with marriage. The hawthorn was dedicated to Hymen (*Hymenaeus*) the god of marriage. It was used as a symbol of a happy marriage and was often used in bridal bouquets not only for this sentiment but because of its pretty flowers.

Hyssop

(Hyssopus officinalis)

Hyssop is a perennial shrub that gets about two feet high with small spiked leaves and purplish-blue flowers. An easy herb to start with stem cuttings that are placed in a glass of water until rooted. It also can be grown by seeds (plant about ¼ inches deep) or you can divide grown plant by the roots and re-plant or pot. It does well in either full or partial sun and tolerates cold better than it does hot. The plant does not like to be sitting in water; rather prefers well-drained soil which makes it a good potted plant. If grown in a garden it is best to thin plants to about 1 foot of space apart.

As like most evergreens, hyssop can be detected by the camphor-like smell. Hyssop is a hearty herb with little white flowers making a great low hedge or border for a garden.

It is said if planted near grapevines it will increase the yield of grapes and if planted near cabbage it will protect the cabbage from cabbage moths which prefer the hyssop over the cabbage. When you want to harvest you will want both the flower tops and the leaves. The flower tops make great teas or tonics. The leaves are also used for making tea or for flavoring soups or salads.

Hyssop is native to the Mediterranean region and is one of the oldest known herbs. The Pilgrims brought it to the "new land" with them when they came to America. It is cultivated in many countries and is used as fragrance in soaps, cosmetics and perfumes.

Hyssop is used to flavor sauces and seasonings as well as the alcoholic drinks of absinthe and chartreuse. It has a strong minty taste and it works well when used sparingly in either herbed butter rolls or mixed with honey.

Did you know?
Hyssop is used after a facelift.

Hyssop has a long history as a medicinal herb. It has an ancient medical reputation and was used for purifying sacred places as well as being used as an antiseptic. Mentioned many times in the bible, this reading from the book of Psalms (51:9) says "Purge me with hyssop and I shall be clean" indicates how long ago it was used. It is still used today either by using fresh leaves or by making a tonic for wounds and bruises after a face lift.

Lavender

(Lavandula angustifolia)

Lavender is an evergreen shrub that gets up to 3 feet tall has narrow green leaves with flowers on a spike in a blue purple color. It prefers a sunny, dry and rocky habitat and is native to the Mediterranean. It is quite hardy. The greatest deterrent is too much moisture and high humidity, which leads to root rot. It is best started from a cutting from another plant. When planting, mix soil with sand to help with drainage and prevent root rot. Leave a lot of room, at least 2 feet for each plant, to allow for growth.

This hardy plant grows well along a sidewalk or driveway as it loves the reflected heat and makes for a nice border. Rose and lavender have always been a popular couple in arrangements and potpourris; maybe because they make great companion plants.

Lavender is aromatic and can be identified by its clean fresh scent that most everyone is familiar with. It is currently the most commonly known herb and has been the most widely used throughout history.

In early England, wash maids would drape the wet clothes over a patch of lavender to dry and absorb the fresh scent. "Lavandula" comes from the Latin "lavare" meaning to wash.

Romans used lavender for bathing, and spread its use throughout their travels. Early Greeks named it "nard". And lavender is mentioned in the bible several times. During the Middle Ages it was one of the strewing herbs, used as an insect repellent and an antiseptic.

It is considered a staple for most herb gardens. Today the flowers are used in pharmaceutical antiseptic ointments; it is a common fragrance in soaps, lotions, perfumes, air fresheners and shampoos; and, is used to flavor food (including frostings and cookies) and alcoholic and other beverages.

Lavender has many culinary uses and the current trend in cookbooks devoted to lavender will attest to that. One of the oldest and easiest recipes to make with little effort and a big payoff is lavender sugar. The sugar can be used many ways and can be flavored with many other herbs than lavender. Sprinkle it on sugar cookies, pastries, scones, bars, pies, cakes; or use as a sweetener in fruit compotes, puddings especially tapioca or rice pudding; sprinkle on ice cream and sorbets and use to sweeten beverages such as tea, fruit juices, or punches.

25

Sweet Marjoram and Oregano

(Origanum marjorana)

A bushy perennial plant (grown as an indoor annual in colder climates) it gets up to two feet high with dark green leaves and small grayish-white or pink flowers. Oregano is the heartier of the two while sweet marjoram is more sensitive and best grown indoors. Both plants prefer full sun and well drained soil. This plant is strongly aromatic and can be identified by smell.

There are three major varieties of marjoram, the two most well-known are sweet marjoram and wild marjoram (commonly referred to as oregano). Sweet marjoram is widely used today within the cosmetic industry and to scent soaps and detergents. Oregano is high in anti-oxidants. Oregano is said to aid digestive and menstrual problems, helpful for muscular and rheumatic pain, sprains, strains, stiff joints, and bruises.

Marjoram and oregano are most known for their culinary talents; particularly in Italian, German, Mexican and French dishes. Italians use oregano with pizza, meat and sauces. The Germans use sweet marjoram to flavor sausage. The Mexicans use oregano in tacos and enchiladas. In French cooking sweet marjoram is used in *Herbes de Provence*.

Did you know:
Marjoram can help you find your future spouse.

Historically, in Greek weddings marjoram was used to bless the wedding couple. Both the bride and groom wore marjoram crowns on their heads and it was used as garland to decorate for the wedding ceremony and on the wedding table. This was the herb of Aphrodite, the goddess of erotic love, beauty, fertility, and marriage. It was believed that if you sprinkled marjoram water on yourself before sleeping you would dream of your future spouse.

Marjoram is sweet smelling (less herbal and more floral) and does make nice water. It is good as a light perfume, for scenting honeymoon sheets, or in an herbal bath or facial mask.

Mugwort

(Artemisia vulgaris)

A perennial herb bush that is grows from 3 to 5 feet tall with purplish stems, dark green leaves with small reddish brown or yellow
flowers. In Northern America it is a hearty weed that attracts butterflies and is an easy to grow embankment shrub that helps prevent erosion.

Mugwort is related to the common wormwood.

It is Native to Eastern Europe and Western Asia where it is still cultivated and used today in soaps and perfumes.

Originally mugwort was use in Eastern Europe in place of hops to flavor beer. A "mug" of beer made of mugwort or wormwood (both are confused and many varieties of each exist) were common in English pubs - hence its name.

Mugwort has no culinary uses as it has toxic properties.

Currently the white fluffy undersides of the mugwort leaves are used in Asia, combined with acupuncture, to combat arthritis. Mugwort is considered an emmena-gogue, or stimulant for menstruation, along with parsley and ginger.

Did you know?
Mugwort can tell your future.

Historically mugwort was used as a protective charm against evil and danger in ancient Europe. It is said that St. John the Baptist wore a girdle of the leaves for protection against evil spirits.

Modern day Wicca's have been known to use it in ceremonies and various love potions. It is thought that if you sleep with a slip of the plant under your pillow you will have prophetic dreams of your future.

Parsley

(Petrosilinum sativum)

Parsley is a biennial leafy plant that grows to a height of two feet tall with feathery and abundant bright green leaves with greenish-yellow flowers. It prefers full sun and moist sandy soil.

Parsley is native to the Mediterranean. It comes in many varieties, but the two most common are curly-leaf and flat-leaf. It is cultivated worldwide for culinary purposes.

Parsley is suited for very fine and delicate dishes. It is high in vitamins A & C, iron and niacin.

The classic French composition of *bouquet garnis* combines a variety of herbs but parsley is always the base.

Fresh parsley also works as a breath freshener.

Did you know?
Parsley will prevent balding.

Parsley is so healthy for you and has such a light flavor that enhances most foods and does not overpower them.

Parsley is also thought to help with bladder problems, arthritis, rickets and sciatica. It is also said to eliminate head lice and stimulate hair growth.

Historically, parsley has been associated with death. In Greek mythology the baby, Opheltes, died on a bed of wild celery. Wild celery, often confused with parsley seemed an evil omen to ancient Greeks. They thought of parsley as a symbol of death and avoided it before a battle. Because of this association it was often planted at gravesites. It, as well as bay laurel, was made into victory wreaths for Olympic winners. You did find it strewn around the floor during the middle ages as it is a natural antiseptic and helped control smells.

Currently it is highly praised for the health benefits it provides. It is considered a diuretic and parsley tea is served in many health spas to relieve fluid retention.

Rosemary

(Rosmarinus officinalis)

Rosemary is an evergreen bush that gets up to six feet high with silvery green spiked leaves with pale blue flowers. The plant if very aromatic and is easily identified by the pine-like smell. It is hard to start from seeds but cuttings will take well. It prefers sandy soil, full light and can withstand drought better than over watering. It works well in a container garden.

Rosemary is native to the Mediterranean and is culti-vated worldwide. Of all the currently popular herbs, rosemary is the most widely used in medicine, cos-metics and cooking. It is used for respiratory, circula-tory, liver congestion, digestive and nervous complaints, muscular and rheumatic pain, skin and hair problems. Currently, it is used in the battle against Alzheimer's and used to restore memory.

It is said to restore luster and shine when used as a hair rinse for brunettes (blondes can use chamomile). Rosemary is used to scent cosmetics, perfumes, and as an insect repellent. Queen Elizabeth of Hungary mixed rosemary and lavender to make a health and beauty tonic called "Hungary Water" thought to reduce the effects of aging and pain of arthritis.

In ancient days sprigs of rosemary were sealed with meat as it flavored and acted as a preservative. The leaves are used in a wide variety of dishes, including fruit salads, soups, vegetables, meats (especially lamb), fish, eggs, stuffing, breads, dressings and even desserts.

Did you know?
Rosemary will improve your memory.

Traditionally, rosemary bouquets were given to the betrothed at engagement parties and young men often proposed with a bouquet as a symbol and gift of their love. Brides carried it in their wedding bouquets to demonstrate their faith and devotion. Grooms wore sprigs tucked in pockets. Guests were given sprigs tied together with a ribbon in remembrance of the wedding. It was burned during the ceremony so that the bride and groom would remember their wedding vows. Wreaths made of rosemary, myrtle and bay laurel were worn by the wedding party and guests.

Rue

(Ruta graveolens)

A perennial that grows to 2 -3 feet tall with small oval shaped smooth leaves with pea green colored flowers with round buttoned seed pods. It survives drought and poor soil better than over watering and a rich soil. It is a very hardy plant and often is used as a border plant. It is propagated by seed or slip cuttings that are allowed to root.

Native to the Mediterranean region, rue is the national plant of Lithuania. Its Latin name translates to "strong smelling," which made it very useful during the Middle Ages to repel flies and mosquitoes.

Did you know?
Rue is a symbol for virginity.

In ancient times it was used as an antidote to poison and believed to be a defense against witches and evil. In the past it was used to treat mental illness because the belief was that the individual was afflicted or possessed by an evil spirit. Individuals with epilepsy were adorned with a necklace made of braided dried rue.

Rue is considered the "herb-of-grace" because catholic priests used it to sprinkle Holy Water on parishioners.

Shakespeare refers to rue in *Richard III:*

"Here in this place
I'll set a bank of rue, sour herb of grace;
Rue, even for ruth, shall shortly here be seen,
In the remembrance of a weeping queen."

In Lithuania, the herb rue symbolizes virginity and repentance. A Lithuanian bride might wear a wreath of rue in her hair as a symbol of her innocence and virtue. During the ceremony the crown is burned symbolizing the bride's movement from young girl to womanhood.

Rue has such a pungent odor and flavor it is very seldom used fresh; however, it makes for a beautiful dried herb. The rounded seed pods are harvested in the fall and are a good addition to a dried floral arrangement either used naturally or spray painted to add color.

Sage

(Salvia officinalis)

A perennial evergreen shrub that gets about 2½ feet tall, with oval shaped soft silver green leaves with deep blue or violet flowers. Growing 1 – 2 feet tall it makes a better outdoor than indoor plant as indoors it can easily get root rot. Outdoors it can easily become bug ridden so pick of pests or spray with a natural pesticide . It prefers full sun and well-drained soil. It is a very fragrant and many varieties are flowering so is great grown near a window or garden sitting area.

Sage is a relative to the mint family. It comes in many varieties (purple sage, variegated sage, and pineapple sage to name a few) with different in colors, tastes, and uses. Garden sage is the most common and generally the one used the most in cooking. The flowering types attract butterflies and hummingbirds.

Sage is native to the Mediterranean region and is currently cultivated worldwide.

Did you know?
Sage means a wise man.

Sage is well known for both the culinary and medicinal uses. It is used for respiratory infections, menstrual difficulties, headaches and digestive complaints. In Medieval times, it was smoked to cure asthma. Sage tea is considered a good blood tonic and a comfort for sore throats and mouth sores.

"Sage" means a wise man and originated from the ancient beliefs that sage promoted wisdom and increased mental awareness. It was also believed to increase sensory perceptions.

Sage has been considered a sacred and healing herb for centuries. It is burned to cleanse an area of harmful spirits and/or bad smells.

Sage is used in flavoring foods, soft drinks, and alcoholic beverages, namely Vermouth and cosmetics. It is a common ingredient in turkey rubs.

Sorrel

(Rumex acetosa)

Sorrel, a perennial, is a hearty plant that grows under almost any conditions. It tends to tolerate the cold weather better than heat and doesn't like to go dry. It will grow to a height of two feet with green oval shaped leaves with red flowers. The seeds are very, very tiny and like to be set about a foot apart. Once settled they are best to propagate by dividing.

Avia Lukacs & Therese Francis

Sorrel leaves can be eaten fresh in salads or cooked as a green. Harvest the leaves when they are young for the best flavor. As the plant ages the leaves become bitterer. It is native to Europe, Asia and America.

Did you know?
Sorrel leaves taste like spinach.

Sorrel is used in flavoring and goes well with fish and egg dishes. It can be cooked much like spinach and is often substituted in recipes. It has a sharp taste sometimes called "sour" which is how it derived the name. Historically there is not much known about sorrel except that it was used fresh in salads.

The flowering spikes are cut off before they seed and can be used for dried flower arrangements, or pressing for cards.

Spearmint

(Mentha spicata)

Spearmint grows to a height of a little over a foot tall and is best grown in a container or it will take over a garden. It prefers a rich moist soil and can tolerate full sun or partial shade. Squared stems with smooth shaped leaves with tiny purple/pink flowers that bloom in mid summer. It grows easily with slips rooted or by dividing and is best started with a plant for your own garden. Once it flowers, cut them in order to produce better tasting mint leaves.

Mints are bright green leafy perennials with square stems. This family contains many well-known varieties such as spearmint, peppermint, pennyroyal, lavender, verbena and borage. All are aromatic and can be identified by smell.

Once native to the Mediterranean, it is now cultivated world-wide. Mint is most well known as a flavoring for toothpastes, chewing gum, candy, alcoholic and other beverages. It is used to flavor cakes, cookies, candy, meats, fruits and vegetables. Mints are known to aid in digestion. Mint tea and beverages are very popular, for example, in France, crème de menthe is a popular after-dinner beverage.

Did you know?
Mint was once believed to be a nymph.

According to Roman mythology, Persephone changed the nymph Minthe into sweet-smelling mint to save her from being raped by Hades. Another legend is that Pluto was in love with the nymph Minthe and ignored his wife. His wife became so jealous she turned the nymph Minthe into a plant.

The Greeks believed that mint was an aphrodisiac and used it in their banquets by mulling it over the tables before serving the food.

Thyme

(Thymus vulgaris)

A perennial evergreen shrub that grows to about 1½ feet high. It sprouts fairly easily from seeds that are not planted too deep. Thyme prefers a little room to grow and should be planted about a foot apart as they are creepers. It grows best in warmer climates or indoors and don't take well to over-watering. Thyme propagates easily by cuttings and will spread quickly. Thyme prefers sun over shade.

There are over 300 different varieties of thyme and each have their own colored blossoms. The plant has a strong pleasant aromatic smell. One of the many varieties, lemon thyme, not only smells the best but is wonderful in cooking and is often found in the kitchen herb pot. Garden thyme has grayish green leaves and pale purple or white flowers and blooms in late summer. Once harvested and allowed to dry, simply run your fingers up the spine and the little leaves will disengage well for preserving. Thyme attracts bees and is said to make the best type of flavoring for honey.

Thyme is a popular culinary herb, often used with fish or poultry.

Did you know?
Thyme was used to preserve mummies.

Thyme is native to Spain. Thymus, the essential oil of thyme, is currently used for medicinal purposes. Both the essential oil and the dried leaves have antiseptic properties.

Early Egyptians used thyme in their mummification process. Greeks and Romans thought it possessed magical qualities and was thought to invoke bravery. In fact, "thumus" is the Greek word for courage. In the Middle Ages, it was thought if you tucked a sprig of thyme under your pillow, it would ensure a good night's sleep.

Verbena

(Verbena officinalis)

Verbena is most often planted in groupings because it is a spindly-thin looking plant. The long hairy stems can reach a height of 3 – 6 feet with the leaves clustered around the bottom of the plant and the blossoms forming a square mound at the top. Verbena does best in rich moist soil and hot sunny days.

Verbena is a perennial plant that is used in landscaping as a border plant to attract butterflies and bees. It will propagate quickly because it reseeds itself. It continues to bloom from spring through to the first frost in warmer climates. In cooler climates it grows best indoors.

There are about 250 different varieties of verbena and is a relative to vervain. The two most popular are lemon verbena and the purple top. This herb is native to the Americas and was first discovered in Argentina and Chile by Spanish explorers. The Spaniards prized it for its aromatic lemony scent and it was (and is still today) used in perfumes, beverages and culinary dishes.

Did you know?
Verbena is the youngest of all known herbs.

Vervain was used by Native Americans medicinally as a relaxant and valued for its sedative qualities.

Lemon Verbena is an aromatic addition to any salads or deserts you chose to serve at your wedding and can be used (like angelica) to decorate the wedding cake or petite fours. Fresh sushi topped with a verbena flower is decorative as well as delicious.

Section 2:
And Now onto the
Wedding Preparations

The second section gives ideas for using herbs in your wedding plans from unique invitations to center pieces for the reception tables.

Wedding Flowers: Boutonnieres, Corsages and Bouquets

The Language of Flowers

The Greeks developed a language of flowers, known as floriography. For example, the cowslip symbolized counsel. In Elizabethan and Victorian England flowers held different meanings. Shakespeare used many in his plays. In this romantic time period the language of flowers and the sending of tussie-mussies was the custom of the times. The language of flowers varies by time period and country.

The language of roses is well known today. Here are some of the most common rose colors and their modern meanings:

Rose Color	Meaning
Red	love, respect
Yellow	friendship, joy
Coral	desire
Lavender	enchantment
Dark pink	thankfulness
White	innocence, secrecy
Pale pink	grace, joy
Orange	fascination
Pale peach	modesty

Wedding Flowers

Whether fresh, dried, or silk, flowers are an important part of weddings. And can be a significant expense, from the bride's bouquet to the groomsmen's boutonnieres.

Boutonnieres are made from a single flower, cut short, that can be pinned to the wearer's jacket or shirt. Corsages are one or several flowers, cut short, and made into a wristband or pinned to a jacket or dress. Bouquets are larger arrangements, with long stems, often with several types of flowers and plants combined together with ribbons or bows. Frequently men wear boutonnieres and women wear corsages, but that's not a hard rule.

Here's a list of possible flowers you will need at your wedding.

Bouquets

Bride

Throw-away (normally made from silk)

Maid/Matron of Honor

Bridesmaid(s)

Flower Girl

Boutonnieres

Grooms

Best Man

Groomsmen

Ushers

Ring Bearer

Bride's Father/Step Father

Groom's Father/Step Father

Grandfathers & Godfathers

Corsages

Bride's Mother/Step-Mother

Groom's Mother/Step-Mother

Grandmothers & Godmothers

Personal Attendant

Others That You Might Include

Guest Book Attendant

Candle Lighter

Readers

Soloists

Organists

Cake Server

Greeters

Other Places That Might Need Flowers

Alter

Pew Bows

Main Entrance

Reception Entrance

Centerpiece for the Head Table

Centerpieces for Guests Table

Cake Table or on the Cake itself

Guestbook Table & Gift Table

Rest Rooms

Buffet Table

Other Flowers You May Want

Flowers for a basket for flower girl

Flowers or wreath for adorning hair

As Gifts to hostesses for various wedding events

As favors for guests

Boutonnieres and Corsages

A simple boutonniere is the easiest to make. It usually consists of a single flower and a few sprigs or leaves as a complement. Some suggestions for a flower are a single rose, carnation or chrysanthemum – usually white or cream colored. Some suggestions for the complement green are sprigs of rosemary or lavender and leaves of mint or sage.

Boutonnieres and Corsages

One fresh flower (boutonniere) or several (corsage)

A complement fresh herbal green

Florists tape

Florist's wires

Ribbon to match wedding

Pearl ended stick pins

Elastic loop (for wrist corsage)

1. Trim the stem of the flower and the complement green to the same size - about 3 inches.

2. Bind the stem of the flower and the complement together (to each other) with the florist wire (just wrap it around both of them). At the end cut off the wire and bend it up and flat against the plants.

3. Cover the stem with the florists tape, winding it upward from the bottom of the stems then downward. Make sure everything is covered well and particularly the cut end of the stem so that it does not bleed later.

4. Tie the ribbon around the base of the boutonniere. Provide pretty pearl ended stick pins to attach.

Use the same process to make a corsage only add another flower or more complement greens. If making a wrist corsage you will need a loose elastic loop that you securely pin the corsage to. The elastic loop needs to be of a loose mesh and you must allow enough room to adapt for sizing to the wrist.

You can label each and store in a cool place, then give to the bridesmaids or groomsmen to distribute the day of the wedding.

Tussie-Mussies

Tussie-mussies – or little bouquets – were thoughtful communications expressing ones emotions and given as gifts. Each flower had a message or hidden meaning.

Little tussie-mussies with your own secret messages would make wonderful bridesmaid bouquets. Choose the flowers by the message you want to send. A single large flower in the middle surrounded by some leafy herbs will make a beautiful looking and smelling bouquet. A nice thank you gift could be a tussie-mussie bouquet weeks after it is all over with a warm thank you note. And, for those that didn't do such a good job – well, you know the secret meanings the tussie-mussie bouquet can hold.

Tussie-Mussies Bouquet

    Fresh flower heads – dried off with paper towels

    Fresh herbal greens

    Florists tape

    Florist's wires

    Ribbon to match wedding

1. Start with a center flowers grouping together as looks the best. If flower stems are not compliant thread a small piece of the wire through the stems to help them hold together better.

2. Then, add the herbal greens. You can do another layer of flowers or greens.

3. Wind the florists tape around all of the stems – tying them together as one. Trim all of the stems so that they are all the same length.

4. Wrap the ribbon around the florist tape so that it does not show. Tie a bow or leave a trailing ribbon.

A fresh bouquet can be made a couple of days before and kept in water and misted occasionally. Take out of the water early enough the day of the wedding so that the stems are not wet. Use a blow drier if you need to dry out.

Laurel Wreaths

Bay laurel is the symbol of eternal love. You can make laurel wreaths for many decorative purposes such as around the matrimonial candle, a platter or punch bowl at the reception, and the wedding cake. Consider adding mini lights with laurel wreaths around table edges, staircase banisters, windows, pews or doorways.

Laurel Wreath

> Cuttings of bay laurel
> Chicken wire
> Sphagnum moss
> Potting soil
> U-shaped floral pins

1. Soak the moss in a bucket of water for several hours.

2. Cut the chicken wire the length of the measured area of your candle and about 3″ wide. Bend the sides up so that it forms a trough.

3. Squeeze the excess out of the moss and pack it inside the chicken wire trough.

4. Moisten the potting soil and add as much as you can into your trough.

5. Using the loose edges of the trough wind together the sides. Sort of squeezing and forming with your fingers until you get the shape you want. Use the additional wire to secure the planting wreath across the breadth every inch or two.

6. Lay the laurel cutting out in an attractive arrangement, planning how you will plant them.

7. Poke a small hole through the moss and through the soil. Put one cutting into each hole. To secure and controls leafs use the U-shaped floral pins.

8. Continue poking and planting until the wreath is covered. Soak well this first time and drain in a sink or bucket.

9. Then hang or set in a sunny area and water lightly when the moss is dry to your touch. Spraying it periodically will keep the leaves fresh and dust free until the wedding.

You should start your wreath at least six weeks before the wedding in order to get it trained to the shape you want. You will have to trim and tuck as it grows in order to prune it to the perfect shape.

Invitations

A unique wall hanging or invitations can be made by pressing dried flowers. The wall hanging is much like botanists of the past used to preserve their identifications.

Many of us have saved the luckily spotted four leaf clover or gifted daisy between book pages. This is the same idea, however to make the final result a little more appealing we will make our own press.

Pressed Flower Wall Hanging

Herbs and flowers, dried

Blotting paper

Cardboard

Tape (masking tape preferred)

Boards

Rubber bands

Wedding invitation or 5 X 7 piece of paper with the wedding details inscribed

1 piece of back drop paper 16 X 20 inches

1 piece of lightweight poster board 16 X 20

Double sided tape

Glue

Wooden frame with glass to fit

Part 1: Press the Herbs and Flowers

1. Place the herb or flower on a sheet of plain blotting paper or other paper that is absorbent and does not have a finish to it. For flowers you may want to dismantle the plant with tweezers placing each petal, stamen, leaf, etc. one by one in place.

2. Top with another piece of the blotting paper.

3. Add a sheet of cardboard, securing it in place by taping the edges to hold it.

4. Slide another piece of cardboard underneath and tape in place.

5. Get two boards and place the contents inside the two boards.

6. Secure the two boards in place with rubber bands.

7. Allow to dry up to 8 weeks. Or to speed up the process, place the press in a microwave oven for about 2 minutes on the defrost setting. Let them cool completely, and, if possible, let them set for a day or two.

8. Open carefully and using tweezers, place your pressed herbs in a flat box or an envelope until ready to use.

9. Label each to easily identify later.

Part 2A: Make a Wall Hanging

1. Glue the background paper to the poster board and allow to dry.

2. Mark off in pencil a boarder of 1 inch or more on the poster board.

3. Glue the wedding invitation to the center of the frame – evenly centered to the border. Or make the center piece yourself using a felt tip marker or inked calligraphy on the 5 X 7 piece of paper.

4. Starting with this bordered area fill in with the dried herbs. The larger dried and pressed whole herbs and flowers work best for this. Fill in spots that look empty with small dried leaf and flower pieces. Use double sided tape to lay items before you glue them. Little glue dots and little foam fixers (sold in craft stores) can make this a much easier process. Glue other herb and flower pieces around the corners and edges of the central invitation.

5. Assemble the glass piece and frame.

Part 2B: Make Invitations

Invitations can be made much the same way as the wall hanging. Guest can frame the invitation as a keepsake.

Or you can buy cardstock ready folded and simply glue your pressed herbs and flowers on the cover of the card.

Wedding Favors, Table Placement Cards and Thank You Notes

Little sachets, potpourri, or thank you seed packets make great favors or gifts for bridesmaids or grooms-men or other attendants.

Lavender and Rose Potpourri

2 C dried and fresh rose petals

½ C dried and fresh lavender blossoms

½ C rose geranium leaves

1 Tbsp fresh lemon peel

1 Tbsp fresh orange peel

1 vanilla bean

Caraway and Citrus Potpourri

1 C caraway seeds

2 C dried citrus peels

¼ C dried cedar chips

1 Tbsp cloves

Keepsake Sachet Packets

White paper, manila envelopes, bridal gift wrap or tissue paper

Glue

Scissors

1 tsp orris root, dried*

Potpourri, either the examples above or a mixture of your own choosing

Fragrance oils*

Orris root and fragrance oil can be found at most craft stores or candle making supply stores.

---

1. Make your own envelope by taking apart a clasp style manila envelope approximately 5 X 7. Carefully unfold the manila envelope and retrace on any paper of your choosing. You can use white paper and then color or decorate to compliment your wedding scheme or use bridal gift wrap.

2. Make potpourri by mixing the dried herbs, flowers, seeds, etc. that you have collected.

3. Add one teaspoon of dried orris root to every two cups of dried herbs and flowers to increase the potency and life of the potpourri.

4. Add some fragrance oil to renew scent after about 4 weeks.

As Table Placement Cards

The packets will make great table place cards for individuals or an entire table. The design should match your invitations or wedding theme. Make the envelopes first, then write the guests names on the envelopes using a calligraphy marker before filling.

As Wedding Favors

Place all the sachet packets together in a decorated basket by the guest book for guests to pick up and take home with them as they sign your guest book.

As Thank You Cards

You can write handwritten messages on them. For example, "thank you for sharing this special day with us" followed by the wedding date and personal signatures. Or mail later as thank you notes for wedding gifts.

Table Center Pieces

A single bough laid on the table can make a simple but elegant table centerpiece or in a more formal arrangement in a vase. They are perfect for a spring wedding since they bloom in May and the white flowers will match any color wedding ensemble. Another great use for the bough is to drape or tie them on the pews of the church – then they can be untied by the bridesmaid's and set on tables as centerpieces at the reception. Here are directions for a braided heart wreath where a bough is used to decorate. The wreath can be hung on the wall, tied to pews or placed flat on a table.

Braided Heart Wreath

> 3/8" & 1/8" satin ribbon to match or accent the wedding colors
>
> Small (6 – 12 inch) size blooming hawthorn bough
>
> 18 gauge floral stem wire
>
> Hot glue & low temp glue gun
>
> 1 package macramé braid – 4mm – any color

1. For each wreath, cut the macramé braid into three 9 inch lengths.

2. Braid these lengths together all the way down.

3. Bend the stem wire into a heart shape.

4. Begin gluing the braid to the wire in the center of the braid and inside point of the heart. Hot glue the wire to the back of the braid, letting the ends hang loose underneath.

5. Next, unravel the ends up to the wire then trim the ends to a uniform length.

6. Tie a short length of ribbon around the unraveled part at the top of the unraveled ends.

7. Glue the bough to the bottom tip of the heart over the unraveled ends; or from the top tip of the heart.

8. Attach with a satin bow to secure.

9. Glue small flowerets where any glue spilled or you need an accent flower.

Before the wedding the bride and her bridesmaids can have a braid making party and each make one in about an hour. It's a great get together with very little real work involved. After the wedding these braided heart wreaths can be given to each bridesmaid as a gift.

Basil Pots

Since basil has such a wide array of fragrant choices and most all have white delicate flowers that will easily adapt to any floral color scheme, it is perfect for adding scent and table centerpieces to your wedding. The effectiveness of the subtle scent will create a pleasant atmosphere for your guests. Include a few fresh sprigs in with your floral centerpieces in the reception area or restroom. Basil is perfect for this as it has so many varieties to choose from. Placed on windowsills or hallway tables they can be unobtrusive yet poignant and can also be used as favors and given to guests to bring home.

Basil Pots

> Basil seeds or seedlings
> Clay pots
> Potting soil
> Ceramic paint
> Spray sealer in clear gloss or antique gold or silver
> Brushes
> Ribbon or rafetta

1. Paint the lip of each clay pot in a color that coordinates with your wedding scheme. Let dry thoroughly.

2. Spray entire pot with sealer and let set for several days before planting.

3. Fill each pot with potting soil and plant either seeds or cuttings.

4. If using seeds they should be planted about 1/8" deep and pack new soil gently over the top. Then cover with clear plastic wrap and allow to germinate

about three days. Then remove the plastic covering. (Basil is easy to grow from seeds. You can also start in something else and then transplant seedlings into clay pots. If sowing seeds you will need to start eight weeks or so before the wedding.)

5. Trim with a rafetta, satin, or gross grain ribbon tied underneath the lip of the pot.

Mix varieties of basil in each pot.

Pots can be painted and trimmed differently to match your wedding scheme. Consider adding your wedding date and names on each pot, and then have guests bring them home as table favors.

If you are using the pots for the aroma, clove is a sexy scent but you will probably have to order it on-line or directly from a greenhouse to find fresh herb.

Add other flowers or herbs to pots for color. For example, rosemary, curly leafed parsley, flat parsley, all the various mint varieties, or marjoram.

For added interest at the reception, use a variety of pots of fresh basil alternating with votive candles on the guest tables. Cluster groups of pots on reception or wedding tables.

Water pots a couple of days before planning to use or provide drain plates if still wet before setting up.

Herbal Ice Blocks

Ice blocks are useful for keeping drinks and *hors d'oeurves* cold, and look great on a wedding party table.

Ice Blocks for Champagne or Wine

Empty milk carton

Empty wine bottle or bottle of vodka

Cold water

Fresh sprigs of mint or flowers

1. Wash a half-gallon milk carton and cut the top off.

2. Add an inch of water and position an empty bottle or bottle of vodka (it won't freeze) in the center of the carton.

3. Add a single layer of mint (or other herbs or flowers) all around the bottle poking them under the bottle.

4. Freeze.

5. Add more layers, being sure to freeze each layer thoroughly so the herbs don't float to the top.

6. When ready to use, peel the carton off and remove the bottle. You may need to drizzle a little warm water over the bottle to soften the ice just enough to get it out.

7. Place on a deep plate or bowl to catch melts and place a bottle of champagne or wine in the center.

Avia Lukacs & Therese Francis

Herbal Ice Bowl Center Piece

2 glass bowls, one that fits inside the other
Cold water

1. Fill the larger bowl with about an inch of cold water.

2. Add herbs and flowers.

3. Freeze.

4. Put a weight in the smaller bowl and place on top of the larger bowl.

5. Add more herbs and flowers.

6. Add water.

7. Freeze.

8. When you want to use, wipe the inside of the smaller bowl with a hot wash rag to release.

9. Dip the bottom of the larger bowl in lukewarm water until it will release easily.

10. Place on a large serving platter or inside a bowl to catch the water as it melts.

This makes a stunning centerpiece and can hold anything that needs to stay cold during the reception or party.

Drying Herbs for Your Wedding

Harvesting can be tricky. Not only do you need to identify the herb properly but you must also catch it or come upon it while it is in the most beneficial harvesting time for the individual plant. To preserve blooms, flowers, stems, petals, etc. cut down on a dry day with a scissor or sharp knife leaving a long stem. Wrap together loosely in a bunch, tie with a rope or ribbon and simply hang up side down in a dry area out of the sun until dry. You can lay them on a shelf, use elastic bands to attach to a coat hanger, or leave in a vase until dried out. An attic works better than a basement because attics hold less moisture.

If you don't want to wait, you can always dry them in an oven or the microwave. Use a cookie sheet, or glass plate if using the microwave, and make sure none of the herbs are touching. Bake at 350 degrees turning periodically to ensure even drying. If using the microwave set at intervals of 30 seconds, checking and re-arranging until done. The niftiest is a food dehydrator it works the best and is the easiest. You put the herbs on the tray and turn it on – no checking - the dehydrator does all the work.

For oven or dehydrated herbs, run a wire through individual flowers before you dry them out and they will be easier to work with once dried. Petals can be pulled apart and allowed to dry individually as well as in little buds and then include some full-fledged flowers in bloom. Some petaled flowers dry best placed in a box of silica gel or orris root powder. Most craft stores sell it. Once thoroughly dried out you can use them to make floral arrangements, wreaths, bouquets, pressed flowers or potpourri.

Don't limit yourself to collecting only the flowers. Grasses, seed pods, sticks, nuts and fruits can also be used. Most decorative grasses, seed pods, stems, roots and seeds or nuts do not need to be hung upside down. They will preserve just as they are. Or, you can spray them with paint to add color or my favorite is a clear spray polyurethane finish. Some ideas of what to collect:

Pinecones

Peppers

Thistles – can be picked as seed pods and will open once dried

Leaves – bamboo and palms and the rich colors of autumn harvested maple and oak

Grasses – reeds, cattails, moss, lichen, ferns, and barley

Flowers – for example,

Dahlia	Tansy
Chamomile	Yarrow
Buttercups	Babies Breath
Snapdragons	Roses
Lilies	Bachelor Buttons
Chrysanthemums	
Calendula & Straw flowers	

The list of flowers is endless - as are the idea's you can create. Dried and pressed flowers between pages of a heavy book is an age old practice we are all familiar with. Place flowers individually and use white tissue to keep a clean imprint on each flower. See the section on sorrel for ideas of what to make with pressed flowers.

Jumping the Broom

"Jumping the Broom" is a wedding ritual found through-out the world. The wedding couple would lay the broom on the floor (or in some traditions, the best man and maid of honor would hold the broom up slightly from the floor – generating a lot of laughs by adjusting the height up and down), hold hands and jump over it together symbolizing their jumping into their new life together. The brooms are often decorated with shells, ribbons, fresh flowers and herbs.

Decorative Broom

> Straw broom
>
> Shell, small rocks or flat marbles
>
> Ribbons, bows (matching the wedding colors)
>
> Glue gun

To make a decorated straw broom, arrange flowers, herbs and ribbons (matching the wedding colors) on to the flat base part of a broom.

Once you find an arrangement you like, use a glue gun to attach the items more permanently.

The broom can be hung on the wall in the new home for wedding memories that will last a lifetime as well as be passed on throughout the years to new brides forming a traditional bond for the family.

Preserve Your Wedding Dress

Lavender is a deterrent to moths and is used in sachets placed in closets and drawers. Lavender wands are a popular replacement for sachets. They are easy to make and great for preserving your wedding gown along with blue tissue paper. The lavender will keep the bugs out and your gown smelling fresh. The blue tissue paper will help prevent the gown from yellowing with age. Stuff the sleeves and gown with the blue tissue paper and lavender wands. There are two different versions of wands that follow; the first one much easier and quicker than the second.

Lavender Wands - One Method

> Lavender spikes with flower buds
> Scissors
> Spool of Ribbon ⅛ to ¼ inch wide matching bridal colors
> Approximately ½ yard of netting to match bridal colors

1. Take lavender spikes, approximately 7 to a bunch that are flowering and roll in a piece of netting that covers the entire spikes and overlaps about 2 inches on the top.

2. Tie a silk ribbon around the netting to keep it rolled up and on the spike.

3. As it dries inside the netting it lasts forever. This is the easiest of wands to make.

Lavender Wands - Another Method

This method is slightly more difficult as it involves weaving the ribbon throughout the spikes and then tying them together. For these you want to use as much of the stems without flowers as possible. Use an odd number of lavender spikes, the most common length uses seven (use 5 for a smaller wand or up to 13 for a longer one).

1. Line the lavender spikes up from the bottom and tie them together tightly.

2. Turn upside down and carefully pull the stems down over the ribbon knot being careful not to break them.

3. Tuck the small end of the ribbon underneath amongst the spikes.

4. Using the long end of the ribbon weave the ribbon over and under each spike working from right to left and starting at the base and working your way up to the top.

5. Tighten past weaves as you go to make a new row.

6. When finished weaving, tie off the ribbon in a knot. You can leave a tail to add a bow, bead or knot to finish.

7. Trim with a scissors any excess spikes or ones that don't fit neatly into the wand.

This method is a little more time consuming than the first version but well worth it when completed. They look great and are good for tucking inside of a box when gifting clothing or inside a basket of homemade goodies.

Section 3:
Pampering with Herbs

With all this work, you need some pampering time. Here's where herbs really shine - and you will too after using these ideas.

Taking Care of Yourself Before You Walk Down the Aisle

Baths scented with herbs have been used for centuries to relax, invigorate or provide for various medical ailments. Before, during or after wedding planning relax with muslin bath bags. Make ahead extra's to bring with you on the wedding night and honeymoon.

You can buy little cotton "tea" bags from most craft stores, co-ops or herb shops; or you can make your own. Then fill with dried herbs. After the bath has filled drop the bags into the water and soak. You can also just drop some dried herbs directly into the bath water but the bath bags make for an easier clean-up.

Plan a get together with the women from your wedding party and have each bring their favorite dried herbs, left over material and ribbon trimmings. You provide some simple refreshments.

Herbal Bath Bags

Remnants of muslin or pre-made muslin, cotton or large paper tea bags

Lengths of narrow ribbons can be coordinated to match your wedding colors

Oatmeal - optional

Almond Meal - optional

Powdered Milk – optional

Mixed dried herbs – the following work the best: rosemary, fennel, thyme, geranium leaves, lavender, mint or bay

Essential oils – optional and boost the affect and scent

1. For each bag, cut out a piece of muslin approximately 4 X 6 inches or 10 X 15 centimeters.

2. Fold muslin in half lengthwise and sew the bottom and side seams to make a sachet. Trim the top edge with pinking shears.

3. Turn the bag inside out (so that the seams are on the inside).

4. In a large bowl mix together equal quantities of oatmeal and powdered milk and sufficient herbs to scent the mixture. Here is where you would add 5- 6 drops of essential oils if desired. Fill the sachets half full with this mixture.

5. Sew or tie matching ribbons around the top of the sachet and leave a big loop on the ribbon. This loop can be hung over the faucet tap so that the bath water will run through the sachet.

The bath bag can be used like a tea bag in the tub. Or it can be used at bedtime as a sleep pillow over your nose and eye area or tucked under the pillow case. If you need to reactivate the scent open one end and sprinkle a little vodka over the herbs and re-close. Some suggestions:

Relaxing herbs: lavender, chamomile, bay, cowslip, hyssop, and marjoram

Stimulating herbs: angelica, citrus, caraway, parsley, rosemary, thyme, verbena

Sensual herbs: basil rose petals, red clover, orange buds, jasmine flowers,

Spiritual herbs: sage and fennel.

Natural Douche

1/3 C dried mugwort

1 Tbsp powdered myrhh or 5 drops myrrh essential oil

1. Steep the dried mugwort in 2 cups of boiling water for 10 – 15 minutes.

2. Add myrrh.

3. Mix well.

4. Strain and allow to cool.

5. Pour into a douche bag and fill with additional warm water until bag is full.

You might also try chamomile, rose petals or jasmine flowers. All of these are said to have a natural aphrodisiac quality.

Brown Sugar Scrub

The following sugar scrub recipe is good for a gentle face scrub or full body exfoliation

½ C brown sugar

2 oz. honey

2 oz. olive oil or any other carrier oil

2 oz. Vitamin E oil

Dried and finely grated orange peel

1 – 2 cloves

½ vanilla bean finely grated or ¼ tsp vanilla extract

1. A coffee grinder will work well for the orange peel and vanilla bean.

2. Mix well and allow fermenting for a day or two.

3. If the brown sugar has absorbed too much oil drain off – if too little add more.

4. Remove the cloves and discard before using.

You can substitute 1 tablespoon mixed dried herbs for the orange peel and vanilla.

You can also add 6 – 8 drops total of essential oils for more scent.

Unlike salt scrubs, which can aggravate any tiny open cut, sugar scrubs are easier on the body.

Herbal Water Spritz

It is easy to make herbal water: simply make a strong herbal tea by adding the dried herb to hot water for an hour, strain, and then cool.

These spritzers are great on a hot day, while working out, anytime you need a pick me up, or before bedtime to relax.

Here are a few suggestions with some of their traditional uses:

Peppermint – energizing, relieves nausea and mental clarity

Lavender – relaxing and repels gnats and flies

Basil – sensual

Caraway – reduces bruising and redness

Marjoram – will relieve a headache

Fennel – detoxifying

Elder Flower – relaxes and diminishes freckles

Sage – relaxing, eases sore muscles and helps balance hormones, PMS, menopause

Angelica – helps with breathing

Bay – energizing and reduces itchy skin and insect repellent

Cowslip – relaxing and clears the complexion and reduces wrinkles

Hawthorn – repels bees

Hyssop – eases burns and kills head lice

Parsley – overall tonic and repels insects

Rosemary – energizing and stimulates memory

Rue – removes warts and pimples

Verbena – relaxing and induces sleep

Thyme – energizing and deodorant

The spritzers or herbal waters can be blended to suit your needs. Most are not strong smelling and therefore they will not fight against any perfume you might be wearing.

These also make great gifts for your bridesmaids.

Astringent

Waters also make great face astringents and are very refreshing. For dry skin add a few drops of rose glycerin or jojoba oil; for oily skin lemon or lime juice and for older skin add chamomile, vitamin E oil and evening primrose oil.

Pampering for Two

After the Party Aaahs

Here's a foot crème for massaging tired feet at the end of a long night of dancing.

Peppermint Foot Cream

> ½ C strong peppermint tea that is still warm and/or 4 - 6 drops essential oils
>
> 2 oz. beeswax
>
> ¼ C extra virgin olive oil (or any other carrier oil)
>
> 2 oz. of vitamin E oil

1. Melt the beeswax in a double boiler or in a bowl over a pan of water.

2. Whisking as you go, slowly add the olive and vitamin E oils to the beeswax.

3. Add the peppermint tea a little at a time, whisking in between to blend. Keep adding the tea until it forms a creamy consistency.

4. Add the essential oils, if using any.

You also can buy ready-made unscented hand cream and add the vitamin E oil and peppermint tea until it is a good blend. The vitamin E is good for your skin and it acts as a preservative to prevent the oils from going rancid.

Sage Sticks for Comfort Cuddling

There are so many varieties of sage all very different in appearance, usage, and folklore but most all contain the wonderful identifying scent. Sage has an earthy aroma that compliments a fire perfectly. Sage fire-burners are great for throwing into the fireplace (or fire pit) on the wedding night or any time. Little fire-burners or herb sticks are easy to make and add an aromatic delight while cuddling in front of the fireplace.

Aromatic Sage Bundles

Simply gather your herb into little bunches and wind together with string to form little logs. Once your fire is blazing throw them on the fire and allow the smell to envelope the room. This is a great way to use up discarded stems or leaves from herbs used for previous projects.

A dozen colorful and great smelling logs placed in a tiny box also make for a great gift to newlyweds and new homeowners. The little logs can be used in a fireplace or burned as incense.

You can also make logs with mint, lavender, bay, hawthorn, elderberry (sticks or twigs), rosemary and thyme.

Herb Massage Oil

  5 oz. oil – Grapeseed, almond, olive or apricot kernel – mixed or alone

  1 oz. vitamin E oil – helps prevent the oil from going rancid

  Dried herbs (1 Tbsp or less)

  (optional) 4-5 drops of one or more essential oils (see ideas for blends in the next section)

  Glass jar, preferably blue or brown colored with tight lid

Mix together in a glass container. Allow to sit in a dark spot for about a week. Strain and bottle.

Use herbs that you have available and make up blends that you and your partner prefer.

Massage Oils for the Honeymoon

Honey is a known aphrodisiac. In the Roman days it was said newlyweds ate honey for the first month of their marriage. Hence, the origin of the word "honeymoon".

Herbs can help create a romantic setting. On the honeymoon night start with a love bath for two soaking in herbal bath bags. Directions on how to make your own are described on page 75.

Follow with a sensual massage with herb massage oil known for its aphrodisiacal properties. The massage oil needs to be made a few weeks ahead so the oil can absorb the herbs scent and properties. Massage oils should be a light scent; don't make them too strong.

The following blends are known for their aphrodisiac properties:

Patchouli, rose petals and basil leaves

Sandalwood, orange blossoms and/or peels, and chamomile flower tops

Patchouli, lemon peel, and chamomile flower tops

Lavender and rose petals

Basil leaves and lemon peel

Sage (works well alone)

Any of the following suggestions will also make great thank you gifts for wedding attendants.

Section 4:
Cooking with Herbs
(Plus More Party Ideas)

Weddings are one of the most celebrated rites of passage, historically and currently. It brings a couple and community together to share in one of life's happiest moments. There are many opportunities to celebrate this joyous occasion, some of the most common include: engagement party, bridal shower, bachelor party, rehearsal dinner or grooms dinner, and the wedding reception. And what's a celebration without food?

General Items

Bouquet Garni

Bay, parsley and thyme are the classic *bouquet garni* herbs, an herbal grouping used to flavor soups and stews. Today there are many additional types of *bouquet garni*.

The *bouquet garni* is only used for flavoring and should be removed before serving.

Ginger root, bay leaves & citrus peel for pork

Parsley, bay, thyme & sage for poultry

Parsley, bay & rosemary for lamb

Fennel, dill & rosemary for fish

Bay, horseradish root, & parsley for beef

Thyme, bay & garlic for beef

Additional ideas for using herbs in cooking are listed in Appendix A.

Herbes de Provence

Herbes de Provence is different than a *bouquet garni*; a *bouquet garni* consists of only three herbs: bay, parsley and thyme and is usually put in a cheesecloth bag for flavoring. *Herbes de Provence* is an herb blend that includes lavender. The famous lavender fields of the Provence region of France is what it is named after.

Herbes de Provence typically uses both sweet marjoram and wild marjoram (also called oregano).

1 Tbsp thyme

1 Tbsp chervil

1 Tbsp rosemary

1 Tbsp summer savory

1 tsp lavender

1 tsp tarragon

1 tsp sweet marjoram

½ tsp oregano (wild marjoram)

½ tsp mint

2 powdered or chopped fine bay leaves

Mix together and put in a jar with a tight fitting lid.

Used on meat, poultry, or fish as a seasoning rub before grilling or baking.

Use to season pasta, salads, soups and potatoes anytime you want a flavorful dish.

Use sparingly and to taste because it is a strong blend.

Herb and Hyssop Butter

The following recipes for herbed and honey butter are a quick and easy way to dress up the wedding menu. Both can be made ahead of time, frozen for up to six weeks and are best if the herbs are allowed to set about two hours prior to using. They go great on everything from toast to pancakes.

Herbed Butter

1 lb butter – quartered

Fresh herbs, finely chopped (parsley, rosemary, thyme, oregano, chives, or marjoram)

1. In bowl mix butter with herbs. NOTE: You can make four different flavored rolls at a time by using quarter sticks of butter and adding different herbs to each portion – approximately 2 Tbsp freshly chopped herbs per quarter portion of butter.

2. Take each batch and place in crocks or sauce dishes for serving. Or, place in plastic wrap and roll up like a sausage.

3. Allow to cool.

4. Cut into thin individual pads and place on plate.

5. Make into little molds if you wish.

6. Garnish with sprigs of any fresh herb.

Hyssop Honey Butter

½ C honey

3/4 C butter, room temperature

2 Tbsp chopped hyssop flowers (or substitute with apple blossoms, cornflowers, bee balm, elderberry blossoms or lemon verbena)

1. Combine honey and butter, mixing until well creamed.

2. Blend in flowers.

This butter will add that extra touch to many different dishes, such as bread, noodles, rice, vegetables, meats, and is so easily done. Make ahead - the rolls freeze well. Herbal butters jazz up prepared packaged foods giving them that homemade taste and look. Imagine basil, oregano and thyme butter on pasta, lovage and garlic butter on rice, or lemon verbena and orange peel butter on muffins, pancakes, French toast or dropped into a bowl of hot oatmeal.

Beverages

We have all heard of Mint Juleps and the currently popular Mojitos. These are very similar recipes but each with a different shot of alcohol - one is bourbon the other rum. Both are popular alcoholic drinks for any event surrounding the wedding.

Mint Julep

4 fresh mint leaves

2½ oz. of bourbon whiskey

1 tsp powdered sugar

2 tsp water

1. Gently smash 3 sprigs of mint against the sides and bottom of a tall glass and then drop in.

2. Add powdered sugar and water. Stir.

3. Fill glass with crushed ice and add bourbon.

4. Top with more ice and mint sprig.

Mojito

2 oz. light rum

Juice of half a lime

2 tsp powdered sugar

2 – 3 mint leaves

Lemon-lime soda

1. Gently smash the mint with the powdered sugar.

2. Squirt the juice of half a lime over it.

3. Place in tall glass, add the rum and stir well.

4. Add ice and lemon-lime soda.

5. Garnish with lime and mint leaf.

These recipes make one glass. To make a pitcher, multiply all by the servings per pitcher.

There are many versions of both of these recipes:

- use different mixes, say club soda or tonic water
- use different rums, such as dark or spicy
- add a syrup to the glass before adding the alcohol, for example mint and sugar

Experiment until you find your favorite.

Non-alcoholic Punch (serves 25)

3 (64 fluid oz.) bottles orange juice, chilled
3 (46 fluid oz.) cans pineapple juice, chilled
1 (.25 oz.) package unsweetened dry lemonade drink mix
1 tsp almond extract
1 C white sugar
1 (46 fluid oz.) can fruit punch drink, chilled
Fresh sprigs of spearmint

1. In a large punch bowl mix all ingredients except fruit punch drink.

2. Add fruit punch drink according to taste and color desired.

3. Add herbed ice mold to keep cold.

Herbal Ice Mold

An herbed ice mold made with mint looks great, tastes great, and as it melts it keeps the punch fresh.

Aluminum ringed Jell-O mold or Bundt pan
Fresh mint sprigs

1. Place fresh sprigs of mint into the mold.

2. Add water to cover well.

3. Freeze.

4. Continuing adding layers, freezing each, until the mold is filled. Be sure each layer is frozen or the mint will float to the top instead of being layered throughout the ice.

5. Add to the punch.

Avia Lukacs & Therese Francis

Tea Time

The English are well known for their afternoon tea. A tea party works well for an afternoon bridal shower or gift opening event. Elegant tea pots, cups and saucers with a variety of teas, honey, flavored sugars, scones, cookies, or breads and you've got the party. It is simple and elegant. If you are hosting the afternoon gift opening you may add any left-over's from the wedding feast.

If the bride has registered for china each of the bride maids can pitch in and purchase a tea pot and serving tray. Suggest to guests that they each purchase a cup and saucer. Then all are given to the bride and she has her own tea set. If not, have each guest bring their own cup and saucer and make a game out of it. When guest arrive have them secretly give their cup and saucer to the host. She hands them out later as she is serving tea. Then have each guests name preprinted on a piece of paper with a blank line where guests write in their guess of the original owners. The one with the most correct guesses wins a prize – a collection of herbal tea bags packaged in a cute tin!

Decorations can be simple. A cute tablecloth with colorful placemats and napkins will suffice. A dried herb arrangement can be the centerpiece in a matching or accent vase and given to the bride as a keepsake.

A Great Cup of Tea

There are two ways to make tea: as an infusion or as a decoction. Herb leaves and flowers tend to lend to infusion whereas roots, stems, bark or seeds to a decoction.

To make an infusion, boil water, shut off the heat and add the herbs to the hot water and steep for 3- 15 minutes, depending on the strength desired.

To make a decoction, add the herb to the water first, then boil the water/herb combination until the liquid is reduced, strain and serve.

Herb Scones

    1 C all-purpose flour

    1 C whole-wheat flour

    Pinch of salt

    ½ tsp baking soda

    2 tsp baking powder

    4 Tbsp butter

    4 t chopped fresh herbs mixed or alone (marjoram, thyme, chives, and parsley work well)

    ¼ C milk, buttermilk preferred

    ½ C nonfat plain yogurt

1. In a bowl mix sift the flours

2. Add salt, soda and baking powder.

3. Cut in margarine.

4. Add herbs, milk and yogurt.

5. Mix to form soft dough.

6. Knead on a floured surface until dough holds together, adding more flour if needed.

7. Roll out and cut with cookie cutter.

8. Place on a greased baking sheet and bake at 425 degrees for 10 – 15 minutes or until golden brown.

Engagement Party Salad

Chickweed is known to reduce the negative effects of alcohol and acts as a tonic to the liver. A salad the night before just might help reduce the hang-over of too much partying. This salad recipe can be used in a wedding menu or would be great for an engagement party served with wine, a variety of sliced breads, a cheese plate, olives, stuffed mushrooms, scallops wrapped in bacon or any other appetizers.

Chickweed Salad

Dressing

¾ C Extra virgin olive oil

½ C Red wine vinegar or ½ C Merlot
   (if using Merlot add 1 Tbsp sugar)

2 crushed garlic cloves

1 tsp fresh finely chopped basil and oregano

½ tsp powdered onion

½ tsp sugar

½ tsp salt

freshly ground black pepper

Salad

5 C fresh greens – chickweed, dandelions, watercress, romaine, escarole and leaf lettuce (a variety is the best)

3 oz. thinly sliced cheddar cheese (substitute any cheese)

3 oz. sliced ham sandwich meat (substitute any lunch meat)

about a cup of edible flowers (see Appendix B)

1. Mix dressing ingredients together in a jar, shake well and refrigerate until use.

2. Wash greens, dry off excess water and tear into bite size pieces.

3. With heart shaped cookie cutters cut cheese and meat hearts out of the slices.

4. Arrange cheese and meat hearts on plate of greens.

5. Garnish with washed and dried edible flowers

Munchies for the Planning Party

A lot of planning goes into a wedding. Here's some ideas to help your brain keep coming up with ideas.

Pesto Sauce

> 2 oz. or so fresh basil
> ¼ cup virgin olive oil
> 2 oz. or so pine nuts
> 2 T minced garlic
> ½ cup freshly grated parmesan cheese

1. Mix all in a food processor or blender.

2. To make a larger quantity keep equal parts basil and pine nuts. If it is too thick add more olive oil.

3. Serve with sliced bread or over pasta.

Tomato Basil Salad

6-8 tomatoes, sliced (such as Romas)

Table onions or capers, sliced fine with greens

1 can pitted black olives, whole

1 small container mozzarella cheese balls (or 1/8 C freshly grated Parmesan Cheese)

½ C extra virgin olive oil

1/8 C apple cider vinegar (or other flavored vinegar or white wine)

1 Tbsp sugar

Minced fresh garlic to taste

Whole fresh basil leaves picked off the stem (or 3 to 5 Tbsp dried)

1. Mix the olive oil with the vinegar, basil and garlic. Set aside and let stand.

2. Slice tomatoes and sprinkle with the sugar.

3. Add other ingredients and pour dressing over all.

Other herbs can be added like chives or oregano. If there is any left overs, add hard salami cut into wedge size pieces, any cold left over green beans and rotini pasta to make a great cold Italian pasta salad.

Bachelor Party Ideas

Traditionally the bachelor party was a dinner where the groom invited his close friends to supper the night before the wedding to celebrate his past and congratulate on the future. Some parties encouraged the guests to bring cash for the groom. This tradition was thought to give the groom a stash of cash to so that he could continue to drink and party with his friends after the wedding when his wife took control of the finances. The traditional poker party allowed him a chance to win his loot.

The bachelor's party is a passing-of-rites ritual that continues today in many different fashions. Often the bridal shower and the bachelor party are held on the same evening (generally a week or two before the wedding these days instead of the night before) and the two groups meet up later at a previously designated time.

Often the best man or a brother will host the party – or plan the occasion and the guests meet at a favorite club or restaurant. A suggestion is to ALWAYS ask the groom what he wants. Many times well intentioned single friends will plan a wild party that appeals to the groom's single friends more than the groom. The bachelor party is meant to be his celebration.

If your groom is to have a party at home here is a simple homemade pizza that can be made ahead and kept in the freezer. Or you could easily add snipped fresh basil to the store-bought variety.

Party Menu

Beer, soda and waters

Pizza (see recipe on the next page)

Two Twelve-Inch Pizzas

- 1 Tbsp brown sugar or honey
- 1¼ C warm water
- 1 envelope (¼ ounce) dry yeast
- 2 C all-purpose flour
- ¾ C natural raw wheat germ
- ½ C Kenyon's Johnny cake white cornmeal (or any other brand)
- 1 tsp salt
- ¼ C olive oil

Topping

- 2 large beef steak tomatoes sliced thin
- 4 oz. freshly chopped basil
- 2 C shredded mozzarella cheese
- ½ C shredded parmesan cheese
- 1 lb Italian sausage
- 1 small onion diced
- 1 lb mushrooms, cleaned and sliced thin

1. In one bowl, dissolve the sugar or honey in water and add the yeast.

2. In a separate bowl, combine flour, wheat germ and cornmeal

3. Allow to sit until the yeast foams slightly (about 5 minutes)

4. Combine flour and salt in a bowl. Pour in the yeast mixture and oil.

5. Knead the mixture, gradually adding flour if needed so that the dough is not sticky. The dough should be smooth and elastic.

6. Shape dough into a ball and put in a large oiled bowl, turning to coat the entire ball with the oil. Cover with a towel and put in a warm place to rise.

7. Allow to rise to about double in size – about 1 hour.

8. Punch down the dough and divide into two balls, knead slightly and throw in the air like a real pizza maker – dust with the white corn meal before rolling out.

9. Roll out into a circle, stretching and patting with rolling pin or fingers.

10. Brown the sausage slightly allowing to remain slightly pink and drain under very hot tap water. Pat dry with paper towel.

11. Divide all topping ingredients in half.

12. Layer each pizza as follows: sausage, basil, onions, mushrooms, tomatoes and cheeses.

13. Let set for 15 minutes before baking at 475 degree oven for approximately 20 minutes.

The Bridal Shower

The maid of honor usually hosts the bridal shower with the help of the bridesmaids. The bridal shower usually has a theme and if the wedding theme is herbs the bridal shower can compliment. Bridal shower themes that can complement the wedding could be Culinary or Honeymoon. The invites can be made with pressed or printed herb designed cards and specify which theme giving guests an idea of what presents to bring. Decorations can use fresh, dried or pictures of herbs dressed for the theme you choose. Games and prizes can match the theme also. And, of course you want a simple menu that will match. Idea's for each are listed below.

Culinary-Themed Bridal Shower

Make simple invites on the computer using simple clip art of commonly known herbs for cooking like parsley, marjoram, oregano – use one for all of the invites or use a different herb for each invite. Add some clip art of cooking utensils mixed with the clip art of the herbs. Announce time, date, etc. and state please bring something for the new bride to use in her *blue and white* kitchen this way letting them know the colors the bride is planning for the kitchen.

If you use a different herb on the invites for each guest you can use it as a game. Require each guest to bring their invitation with them to the shower. At the end of the shower have the bride pick the piece of paper that has the herb listed on it out of a hat, basket, etc. and she chooses the grand prize winner. Keep a list of what you gave to each guest so that if they have forgotten theirs - they can still win the grand prize drawing. This should be the herbal centerpiece that you used for the shower.

A cute and economical centerpiece is to cut fresh herbs purchased at the local grocery store and dollar store cooking utensils (wooden spoons, spatula's, soup ladle etc.) mixed together and tied with a ribbon (in the wedding colors) and placed in a simple vase. Fresh herbs can be placed in a teapot, soup urn, canister set, utensil holder, etc. If fresh herbs are out of the question, buy some dried ones and make a potpourri arrangement in a serving dish, cute basket, casserole dish or cookware that has been lined with dish cloths or towels and tie with a ribbon.

Decorations are best left simple and can be dried potpourri, various cookbooks, fresh herbal pot plants, wreaths, *bouquet garni*'s or *Herbes de Provence* jars that you have made. These can also be the prizes the guests win for the games you play.

Games don't have to be elaborate but you should play a couple at least - especially if guests don't know each other. Games usually help break the ice and encourages mingling. Much of the idea of holding a shower in the first place is so that wedding guests can get to know each other a little before the wedding. Some ideas:

Simple seek and find, crossword puzzles or scrambled letters (make your own or do a computer search)

Have each guest bring their favorite recipe on a 3 X 5 card but without saying who it is from. As they arrive keep list each guest and their recipe on a separate 3 X 5 card. Then place only the recipes in a 3 X 5 picture album. Circulate the picture album and have each guest try to guess who brought which one. The one who guesses the most correctly wins a prize. You can then place the separate guest list with corresponding recipe card in the album and give to the bride.

Blindfold and guess game. Place herbs fresh or dried in little bowls on a tray. Not more than 3 – 6 or it gets to be too many smells and a lot of sneezing. Blindfold everyone and walk around letting them guess the herbs by smell only. Then make them write down what they think they have identified. Again, a prize for the winners.

Everyone knows this one – The Newlywed Game. It is old but tried and true and the best ice breaker because it gets everyone telling stories. Ask the bride and groom questions ahead of time such as their favorite song, first date, where they met, favorite restaurant, most embarrassing moment on a date, how the proposal came about etc. and write the answers down. At the shower ask guests the questions and see who answers the most questions right. Again a prize for the winners.

Honeymoon-Themed Bridal Shower

If they have a honeymoon planned use the destination as a theme. If not, you could make it a sexy romantic shower theme; or inspire local area activities that they can visit together after the wedding. For example, movie tickets, baseball games, museums, art galleries, movie rental coupons and restaurant gift certificates. That way if they are not going on a honeymoon they still get to get out affordably or stay in and have fun.

Again, make simple invites on the computer using available clip art of idea's to visit, restaurants in the area, honeymoon location if they have one, sexy old fashioned pin-up girls, etc. Once again use one clip art for all of the invites or use a different one for each invite. And, don't forget to add some clip art of herbs if that is the wedding theme. Announce time, date, etc. and state please bring something for the new bride to use on her honeymoon night in Las Vegas (as an example if appropriate) - announcing the honeymoon plans and if the bride wants lingerie you should note that they can call you for her sizes. If she is allergic or has a favorite-only perfume you should list those simply stating her preferences.

It is best to keep a shower menu simple because you as the host want to be able to mingle with guests, mc games, and refresh beverages as needed. You can ask each of the bridesmaids and mothers of the wedding couple to make a dish and bring with them – this is not only economical and time saving but also allows everyone to contribute.

Shower Menu

An assortment of cold tea, waters and soda beverages

Hot teas and coffee to go with desert.

Salads – how many depending on guest list

Luncheon loaf

Fresh vegetable tray

Chocolate cake

Luncheon Loaf

The luncheon loaf is as simple to make as sandwiches and just a little more time consuming, but looks very elegant. It is basically layers of different breads with different layers of salads in between and then frosted with cream cheese and garnished with fresh herbs. I have listed my favorite but you can change the individual layers to suit your guests if say they are vegan - leave out the ham salad layer and replace with a veggie mix of sprouts, avocadoes, tomatoes, onions and ranch dressing. You can make one layer a soft cheese spread with an herbal butter, or mix diced apples, chopped walnuts and green olives and cheese. Other choices are tuna, shrimp, crab or smoked salmon salad.

It's OK to make the loaf the day before the party, but it is best to frost the loaf the day of the event. Allow enough time for the frosted loaf to sit in the refrigerator for at least 2 hours (this helps it keep its shape and will make it easier to cut) and then at room temperature for at least 20 minutes before serving.

Ham salad (see below)

Pineapple & pecans spread (see below)

Curried chicken salad (see below)

Softened butter

1 loaf bread – unsliced – or ask bakery to slice horizontally into 4 quarters

2-3 (8 oz.) packages of cream cheese

Milk

Fresh herbs and vegetables to garnish

Ham Salad

1½ C chopped (or ground in food processor) ham

2 Tbsp grated onions

¼ C diced dill pickles or sweet pickle relish

¼ C mayonnaise

Pineapple & Pecan Spread

1 C toasted and chopped pecans

1 can (8 ¾ oz.) crushed and drained pineapple

3 oz. cream cheese

Chicken Salad

1½ C cooked and chopped (or ground in food processor) chicken

2 Tbsp grated onion

1 tsp ground curry powder

¼ C finely diced celery

¼ C mayonnaise

1. Make all of your fillings and set aside.

2. If needed slice bread horizontally into quarters. Remove the crusts from the sides and top, leaving the bottom crust. (This will help your loaf to hold together)

3. Starting with the bottom crust, spread each side of the bread that will be touching a filling with butter.

4. The first layer should be the chicken salad.

5. Then again a buttered bread slice.

6. Then the pecan and pineapple spread.

7. Then again a buttered bread slice.

8. Leave the ham salad for the top layer. This order of assembly helps the loaf to hold together better and slice easier.

9. Wrap the loaf tightly, squeezing it softly as you go to shape, with saran wrap and refrigerate for several hours.

Frosting the Loaf

1. Whip the 2 packages of cream cheese with the milk until creamy and of easy consistency to spread.

2. Unwrap the sandwich loaf.

3. Frost with the cream cheese while still chilled.

4. Using a pastry bag you can decorate the top of the loaf just as you would a cake.

5. Garnish with fresh herbs, hard boiled eggs, veggies or olives.

6. Place a wet towel over all and refrigerate a minimum of two hours before serving.

7. Let stand at room temperature approximately 20 – 30 minutes before slicing to serve.

Feeding Visiting Relatives

Here is a great appetizer entry that serves well with a cheese and cracker platter and stretches economically and easily to serve a crowd by adding more potatoes.

Slow Cooker Kielbasa Stew

½ to 1 lb kielbasa (or Polish) sausage cut into 1 inch pieces

½ to 1 lb smoked sausage cut into 1 inch pieces

1-½ lbs sauerkraut (in jar)

2 apples, peeled, cored and sliced into 1 inch pieces

1 small white onion diced

2 lbs red potatoes, washed, and quartered (and peeled if desired)

1-½ C chicken broth

1 tsp fresh or ½ t dried caraway seeds

(optional) ½ C dried cranberries

1. Brown the sausages, drain off grease and pat dry with paper towels.

2. Place in bottom of slow cooker.

3. Cover with remaining apples, onion and potatoes.

4. Pour chicken broth over the combination and sprinkle with caraway seeds.

5. Cover and cook on high for approximately 4 hours or until potatoes are tender.

Another great recipe, this one goes well as a side dish to the Kielbasa stew or for the wedding feast to be served with a pork loin.

Bavarian Red Cabbage

1 small head red cabbage, washed, cored and finely sliced

1 medium onion chopped

3 tart apples, cored and quartered

2 tsp salt

2 tsp caraway seeds

1 C hot water

1 Tbsp brown sugar

½ C apple cider vinegar

3 Tbsp butter

Place all ingredients in the crock pot and cook on low for 8 – 10 hours.

A dollop of sour cream in the center is great garnish.

Rehearsal Dinner

A rehearsal dinner, also known as a groom's dinner, historically was held on the wedding eve in order to chase away evil spirits. Today it serves a more useful purpose gathering all involved to rehearse, ensuring the wedding ceremony will go off well. A rehearsal dinner is held after the wedding party and officiate have gone through all the necessary details for the ceremony itself. The dinner can be held at a restaurant, private home or the location of the wedding. The dinner is usually hosted by the groom's family. Bay lends itself well to beef and here are two rehearsal dinner menus: one for a formal dinner held at home and one for an informal church rehearsal dinner.

Formal Rehearsal Dinner Menu

Tossed salad with herb salad dressing

Prime rib with horseradish sauce

Baked asparagus

Dinner rolls

Poached pears

Prepare the salad, dressing, and asparagus ahead of time. The prime rib can be slow cooked in the oven and the poached pears can be made in the crock pot. Heat the asparagus in the oven while preparing the table and allowing the prime rib to stand before slicing.

Prime Rib Roast of Beef

Prime rib
Salt & pepper
½ C flour

1. Let the prime rib stand at room temperature about ½ hour before roasting.

2. Wipe, rub with salt, pepper, and flour.

3. Place fat side up (or if roast is very lean use toothpicks to cover with pieces of bacon or cabbage leaves) in open roasting pan without water.

4. Place in very hot oven (400 – 500 degrees) and sear 20 minutes until lightly browned.

5. Reduce heat to slow oven (250 – 300 degrees).

6. Add a little water to the roasting pan along with 1 – 2 bay leaves in the water.

7. Roast 16 minutes to the pound for rare, 22 minutes to the pound for medium and 30 minutes to the pound for well done.

8. Baste while cooking to keep the roast moist.

9. If you used bacon or cabbage leaves, remove (and discard) them for the last 20 minutes of cooking.

Use a meat thermometer to ensure that the meat is cooked all the way through. Allow to set before slicing.

Informal Rehearsal Dinner Menu

Sodas and waters

Roast beef sandwiches

Relish tray & chips

This is economical and easy to bring to the church and serve. A cooler with ice and drinks, crock pot with roast beef, buns and cheese slices, relish tray and chips with paper picnic staples. Serve with pre-sliced Submarine, Kaiser or other buns and sliced provolone cheese and pickled pepperoncini's.

Crock Pot Roast Beef Sandwiches

2 strips of bacon

3 lbs. Beef rump or chuck roast (¼ pound per person)

1 medium onion diced

1 10 oz. can beef broth

6 Roma or 3 large tomatoes chopped

2 cloves garlic minced

1 tsp thyme

1 tsp oregano

1 Tbsp basil

1 whole bay leaf

1. Brown the bacon and cast aside. Brown the roast in the bacon grease.

2. Mix all of the other ingredients in crock pot. Add the roast.

3. Cook on high for 1 – 2 hours. Mix or pull apart the roast as it is cooking.

4. Turn to low and cook for 6 – 8 hours, adding water if needed.

The Incredible, Edible Flower

Many of the flowers from herbs and plants can be eaten, for example:

Carnations	Bachelor Buttons
Lilacs	Chrysanthemums
Mint	Nasturtiums
Cornflower	Verbena
Heather	Orange Blossoms
Pansy	Jasmine
Lavender	Cowslips
Elder	Hawthorne
Violets	Snap Dragons

Sometimes a specific color is wanted, other times a specific taste. Appendix B has a chart with common flowers, their most common colors, and tastes.

Edible flowers brighten up a wedding table, meal, salad, cake, etc. They can be served alone as a salad or desert. When harvesting for yourself you need to be sure not to pick plants that have been sprayed with pesticides always wash and dry them before using. You also want to pick later in the day when the sun has already dried off any dew or moisture. You also don't want to use flowers purchased from a florist unless you know they did not use spray. The edible rose petal recipe below makes a great desert alone; as an accompaniment to the wedding cake slices; or sprinkled over sorbet or pudding.

Candied Rose Petals

> Freshly picked rose petals (or any of the edible flowers or mint leaves) dried off
>
> Egg whites
>
> White Sugar (or rose or lavender sugar)
>
> Waxed Paper for drying

1. Whip a couple of egg whites until frothy but does not form peaks yet.

2. Dip the whole flower, petals or leaves - whichever you choose into the egg white and then sprinkle and lightly roll in the sugar. You don't need to have the petal drenched with egg white – just wet slightly.

3. Set aside to dry on the wax paper. If the paper sticks, just peel off.

Candied Angelica

The candied angelica pieces can be cut in varying lengths and rolled in green-colored sugar to decorate a wedding cake, working as stems for crystallized flowers.

It is time consuming but well worth the awe guests will express over the artistic creativity.

> Young stems and stalks of angelica, cut into 2-3" lengths
>
> 1 pint boiling water
>
> 4 oz. salt
>
> 1½ lbs sugar
>
> 1½ pints water

1. Add the salt to one pint of boiling water.

2. Place the stems in a basin and pour the solution over them.

3. Cover with a cloth and leave for 24 hours to soften the stems.

4. Drain and peel the angelica stems.

5. Wash them in cold water.

6. Make a syrup from the sugar and the 1½ pints of water.

7. Bring to a boil for ten minutes.

8. Place the angelica in the syrup and boil for another 20 minutes.

9. Lift out and drain for four days on a wire rack.

10. Reserve the sugar syrup (you will use it in four days).

11. After the four days, re-boil the angelica in the same sugar solution as you did before.

12. Drain and for four more days let set on a wire rack. Or if you have a food dehydrator it can speed up the entire process.

13. Sprinkle with sugar (that's had food coloring added) or dip into melted chocolate.

14. Dry and store in airtight containers.

The Wedding Cake

Ancient Romans and Greeks would make their wedding cake out of wheat or barley and other grains of the times. It was a symbol of fertility and prosperity. At the Greek wedding they would pile up several small cakes on top of one another and have the groom and bride kiss over the tower of cakes. If they managed to kiss without knocking down the tower of cakes it meant a successful union. The tiered wedding cake originated from this tradition. The Roman wedding made a simple cake out of flour, salt and wheat flour. They would shower the bride and groom following the ceremony with cakes instead of the currently traditional rice. This custom was hoped to instill fertility for the couple as wheat was considered a symbol of fertility. Eventually the showering of the cake turned to the wedding couple eating the cake and the tradition of the bride and groom feeding each other the first bite. This symbolizes the sharing of their new lives together.

Wedding cakes remained quite simple until the Victorian era when cakes and customs became more elaborate. One custom in England was to hide a ring in the cake. The guest that found the ring in their piece of cake was to be ensured good luck for a year.

Nowadays, wedding cakes vary according to the bride and groom's favorites - anything from white traditional to vegan cakes are popular. I recently attended a wedding where the bride asked female guests to bring their favorite homemade cake in lieu of a gift. It was great, there were many cakes to choose from and all tasted fantastic. This was one less task for the bride to worry about, the guests saved money and most importantly it encouraged mingling amongst the bakers and tasters!

Small crystal bowls or trays holding candied angelica stems or candied flowers and peppermint cream mints are a nice addition to the cake table; particularly cute if you've decorated the cake with them also. Angelica stems can also be used as swizzle sticks for coffee or tea. Or make the following traditional white cake recipe and deviate to your own tastes. Use a flavored filling for color; add white chocolate, raspberry or banana cream or your favorite flavor. My favorite is a raspberry filling, white frosting topped with crystallized mint leaves, angelica stems and garnished with fresh raspberries.

Basic White Wedding Cake: Two Layer Version

To make a tiered cake you will need more layers of different sizes – two layers for each tier in 10", 8" or 6" rounds. And, you need something to hold the tiers up. For example, you can purchase the plastic column type at most catering or party stores. You could also use plastic champagne glasses (or any decorative glasses) turned upside down.

Two Cakes

    6 C sifted cake flour

    2 Tbsp baking powder

    1½ C butter or margarine

    3 C sugar

    2 C milk

    1 tsp vanilla extract

    12 egg whites

1. Preheat oven to 325 degrees.

2. Grease bottom of pans and line with waxed paper or parchment paper.

3. Sift together flour and baking powder. Set aside.

4. Cream butter and sugar together until light and fluffy. Set aside.

5. Beat egg whites until stiff. Set aside.

6. With mixer at slow speed, add flour mixture to butter mixture, alternately with milk. Beat well after each addition.

7. Add vanilla extract.

8. Gently fold egg whites into batter.

9. Pour into prepared pans.

10. Bake until toothpick inserted into center comes out clean. About 20-25 minutes.

While the cake is cooling make the frosting.

White Frosting

2 Tbsp flour
1 C milk
1 C (2 sticks) unsalted butter
1 C confectioners' sugar
1 tsp vanilla extract (or other for flavoring)

1. Over medium heat cook flour and milk and stirring constantly until thickened. Let cool in a bowl.

2. Cream together the butter sugar and flavoring until light and fluffy.

3. Add the flour mixture beating until mixed well and fluffy.

Raspberry Filling

1½ C frozen raspberries or 2 C fresh raspberries
1 Tbsp cornstarch
2 Tbsp lemon juice
¼-½ C sugar (more or less to taste)

1. Mix all ingredients.

2. Bring to a boil over medium high heat.

3. If not of thick enough consistency, take a little out of the pan, blend in more cornstarch – 1 teaspoon at a time– and then return to the pan. Repeat until thick enough.

Putting the Cake Together

1. Remove cakes from pans and brush off excess crumbs.

2. Place lower layer on plate, bottom side down, and frost with a thin filling about ½ inch.

3. Add filling (optional).

4. Add the top layer of the cake.

5. Drop tablespoons of frosting randomly across the top of that layer. Then spread frosting with a spatula working from center to edges.

6. Frost the sides of both cakes, turning the cake plate as you go around the cakes.

7. (optional) Decorate with candied roses, colored frosting, or commercial decorating kits.

Alternatives to a Wedding Cake

My daughter served a variety of pies at her wedding rather than the traditional wedding cake. She had certain guests (mothers, aunts, cousins, etc.) make and bring their favorite pies and had a few on hand in case guests forgot theirs. A pie was placed at each table after the meal. Guests were instructed to mingle amongst the tables to find the piece of pie they wanted. It was a great ice breaker that started guests mingling after dinner.

Lavender Strawberry Cream Pie

Vanilla Wafer Pie Crust

> 2 C crushed vanilla wafers
> ½ C of melted butter

1. Combine and press over bottom and sides of a 9" single pie pan.

2. Bake at 400 degrees for ten minutes.

3. Remove from oven and let cool.

Filling

> 1 box (8 oz.) vanilla pudding mix
> 4 C washed and hulled fresh strawberries
> ½ C lavender sugar
> Whipping cream

1. Wash and hull the strawberries cutting them in half and sprinkle with lavender sugar and set aside.

2. Prepare the vanilla pudding mix according to decorations for pie filling.

3. Fill pie crust with strawberries and pour pudding over the top.

4. Allow to cool and top with left over whole strawberries and whipping cream.

Lavender, Rose or Mint Sugar (makes about 1 cup)

Some other combinations are:

- lavender sugar with either peaches or pears,
- rose sugar with cherries, blueberries or nectarines and a tapioca pudding mix, or
- mint sugar with raspberries and a chocolate cookie crust

Herbal Sugars

1 C white sugar
1 C organically grown lavender - use flowers and leaves (substitute organic rose petals for rose sugar or mint leaves for mint sugar)

1. Mix in a plastic zip lock bag or glass jar.

2. Seal and let set for 3 – 5 days.

3. Open and sift out the flower petals.

4. Store sugar in an airtight container.

The Wedding Toast

A Non-Alcoholic Toasting Drink

Elder flower champagne is delightfully fizzy yet is a non-alcoholic drink. It is hard to detect the difference - a great alternative for wedding guests. Attach a thank you card and give to groomsmen and bridal attendants.

Elder Flower "Champagne"

> 8 heads of elder flowers
>
> 8 pints boiling water
>
> 1-¼ lbs white sugar
>
> 2 Tbsp white wine vinegar or white wine
>
> 2 lemons, sliced

1. Place the elder flowers, sugar, vinegar and lemons in a very large bowl or wine making drum.

2. Pour boiling water over the mixture, and stir the mixture to dissolve the sugar.

3. Cover the bowl or drum and let stand in a warm place for 24 hours.

4. Strain the liquid into a jug (you will need to do this gradually just pouring a little at a time and waiting for it to clear) or into any clean bottle.

5. Seal the bottles with corks or caps and store in a cool dark place for about 2 – 3 weeks.

6. Serve chilled.

You can add your own personalized labels by either making them on the computer or by hand using sticky labels. Add a ribbon or a bow. Again, match your wedding theme, invitations, etc. Great bottled on the table for guests to enjoy at your wedding or to take home as a keepsake. Or serve in a punch bowl with herbal ice cubes or herbal ice ring described under spearmint.

Toasting the Couple

And, what about toasting? Traditionally, wine has been served at weddings and it is still the most popular beverage served today. A traditional toast, the glasses clinked and the cup emptied is usually how it goes. It originally really did involve toasted bread. In olden days wine left much more sediment than it does today therefore a piece of toast was placed in the bottom of the glass to catch the sediment hence, "toasting". The clinking of the glasses was thought to run off the evil spirits. And it was considered good taste to empty the glass or "bottoms up".

Usually the best man signals the start of dinner by offering a toast to the bridal couple. The maid of honor follows and then parents, any of the bridal party and guests. The best man is really the only one on the spot to start things off. Everyone else can either toast or not toast. Toasting can be humorous, serious, or romantic, often involving the story of how knows the couple—anything to get the party started.

Wedding Feast

There are numerous traditional wedding feasts. Here are a few of my favorites.

Wedding Feast - Lamb

All parts of fennel are edible and popular in today's cuisine. Fennel tastes like black licorice and the seeds are used in flavoring. Heat destroys the flavor of the fennel leaves and care should be taken not to add for any lengthy cooking times. It is best whole or ground and is used in desserts, breads, cakes, cookies and beverages. The stalk is eaten like celery and sliced or minced and added to salads or soups. Ground fennel seeds are delicious in tomato soup. Fennel goes well with fish, sausages, duck, barley, rice, cabbage, sauerkraut, beets, potatoes, eggs and cheese spreads. A wedding feast menu and recipe for roast leg of lamb follows.

Wedding Feast Menu

Orange and mint salad (appetizer)

Roast leg of lamb with Fennel butter

Herb jelly

Bavarian red cabbage (served hot or cold)

Dinner rolls

Wedding cake

Orange Mint Salad

2 – 3 oranges peeled and sectioned (or purchase the canned mandarin and drain)

½ C sweet white wine

2 Tbsp honey

Whole fresh mint leaves

1. Mix the honey and wine together.

2. Warm in the microwave to blend.

3. Garnish the oranges with the mint leaves and drizzle the dressing over the top.

Roast Leg of Lamb with Fennel Butter (Serves 6-8)

Seasoned Butter

    6 Tbsp butter at room temperature

    2 Tbsp Dijon mustard

    1-½ tsp dried crushed rosemary or ½ t fresh rosemary

    3 Tbsp fennel seeds, crushed in a plastic bag with a mallet

    1-½ Tbsp soy sauce

    3 large garlic cloves minced

Mix all ingredients with a fork in a medium bowl and set aside.

Lamb

    2 Tbsp olive oil

    1-1/3 C chicken broth

    1 Tbsp coarsely ground black pepper

    1 6-pound bone-in leg of lamb, well-trimmed.

    2 C dry red wine (merlot works well)

    (optional) fresh rosemary sprigs

1. Position rack in bottom third of oven and preheat to 450 F.

2. Pour olive oil into large roasting pan.

3. Place pan directly atop two stovetop burners over medium-high heat.

4. Sprinkle lamb with salt and pepper.

5. Add lamb to pan and brown on all sides, about 10 minutes.

6. Remove pan from heat.

7. Brush lamb with half of seasoned butter.

8. Roast lamb 30 minutes.

9. Reduce heat to 350 degrees. Continue roasting until thermometer inserted into thickest part of meat registers 130 degrees for medium-rare, about 40 minutes longer.

10. Transfer to platter; tent with foil.

11. Let stand 20 minutes.

12. Skim off fat from drippings in roasting pan.

13. Place pan atop two stovetop burners over high heat.

14. Add wine and broth.

15. Boil until mixture is reduced to 2 cups, about 15 minutes.

16. Whisk in remaining seasoned butter (sauce will be thin).

17. Season sauce to taste with salt and pepper.

18. Garnish lamb with rosemary sprigs and serve with sauce.

Wedding Feast - Fish

Here's another wedding feast combination. Parsley or dill or both combined added to a plain white sauce dresses up baked trout or a salmon loaf. A salmon loaf sliced and a dollop of white parsley sauce is a light and economical wedding entrée. The recipe I have listed will serve 6 and can easily serve more by making more loaves or tripling the recipe and baking in a 13 x 9 x 2 pan. Slice about ½ to 1" thick.

Wedding Feast Menu

Stuffed mushrooms (appetizer)

French onion soup with herbed croutons and Swiss cheese

Salmon loaf

Creamed peas

Lemon rice

Easy dinner rolls with herb butter

Stuffed Mushroom Appetizers (serves 6)

1 lb mushrooms

2 – 3 Tbsp butter

½ C Italian bread crumbs

1/8 C grated Parmesan cheese

2 Tbsp minced fresh parsley

1. Cut stems off mushrooms and dice up fine.

2. Sauté diced mushrooms in butter for 4 – 5 minutes

3. Add Italian bread crumbs

4. Add Parmesan cheese and parsley

5. Mix should be moist if too dry add more butter

6. Stuff mushroom caps and lay out on a broiler pan

7. Broil for about 7 – 9 minutes until stuffing is golden brown.

8. (optional) Add chopped fine oysters, garlic, scallops, pepperoni, jalapeno peppers, onions, browned sausage.

French Onion Soup

1 Qt beef bouillon or broth
3 C thinly sliced Vidalia onions
¼ C butter
¼ C brown sugar
2 Tbsp flour
1 bay leaf
¼ C dry vermouth or white wine
1 C grated Parmesan cheese for garnish
Croutons for garnish

1. Pour bouillon or broth and bay leaf in crock pot, cover and set on high.

2. Sauté onions in butter until transparent. The longer the better for the sweetest flavor.

3. Add salt, sugar, flour and vermouth.

4. Stir well and add to crock pot.

5. Cover and cook on low 6 – 8 hours.

6. Garnish with croutons and cheese.

Salmon Loaf

¼ C milk

2 – 3 C crushed saltine crackers

¼ C melted butter, cooled

1 can (14 ¾-ozs) salmon (drain, wash, pick out bones and skin if present)

1 Tbsp onion powder

1 tsp lemon pepper

2 egg yolks beaten

2 egg whites stiffly beaten

1 – 2 lemons to slice for garnish

1. Preheat oven to 350 degrees.

2. Mix milk, crackers and butter. Set aside

3. Clean the salmon and sprinkle with the onion powder and lemon pepper. Set aside.

4. Add the beaten egg yolks to the cracker mixture.

5. Stir in the salmon.

6. Fold the stiffly beaten egg whites in to all.

7. Pour into well-greased loaf pan.

8. Steam or bake in a pan of water for 40 – 50 minutes until firm or a knife comes out clean from the center.

9. Let stand 5 minutes before inverting on serving plate.

White Parsley Sauce

    2 Tbsp butter
    2 Tbsp + 2 tsp flour
    ½ tsp salt
    1 C milk
    3 Tbsp dried parsley or 2 Tbsp freshly chopped parsley

1. In a 1 quart glass dish mix butter, flour and salt.

2. Microwave on high 2 minutes – stirring after one minute.

3. Gradually stir in milk, adding a little at a time.

4. Microwave on high 3 to 4 minutes – stirring after each minute until thick and bubbly.

5. Cool slightly.

6. Fold in parsley.

I love to make white sauce in the microwave because it always turns out and it is so quick and easy. The salmon loaves can be made ahead and frozen and it slices well for prepared individual servings when frozen. It can be served cold or hot but I prefer it warmed. The white sauce should be made fresh.

This sauce is great drizzled over an entire salmon loaf or individual slices reserving some sauce for on the side with lemon slices and fresh parsley sprigs for garnish. Rice of any kind, pilaf, wild, brown or white goes well with it. I love lemon rice the best. Simply make brown or white rice and before serving add grated lemon peel to taste.

The basic white sauce can be made and anything can be added for variations. Dill can be used in place of the parsley; grated fresh horseradish to accompany beef or lamb; or curry over chicken breasts. I've added fresh cooked pea's to the white sauce. For a more casual dinner I've used tuna instead of salmon and topped the loaf with cheddar cheese.

Easy Dinner Rolls

> 1 package premade cook and serve dinner rolls
> Egg white
> Caraway, poppy, cardamom, sesame seeds

1. Before cooking, brush with the egg white and sprinkle with any one of the seeds or a mixture of the seeds before baking.

2. Bake the dinner rolls according to package directions.

3. Serve with herb butters.

Wedding Feast – Goose or Turkey

Historically, goose was traditionally served at weddings because the gander, always faithful to his original mate, became a symbol of marriage and fidelity.

Wedding Feast Menu

sage cream cheese spread on crackers (appetizer)

roasted goose or turkey stuffed with mashed potatoes

wild rice stuffing

baked sweet potatoes with cinnamon nutmeg butter

rolls

wedding cake

The following herbal blend goes well with stuffing, poultry or fish, and is especially great as a rub for grilled goose or turkey. The recipes below uses fresh herbs but dried can be substituted. Remember that dried herbs have a much stronger flavored than fresh herbs, so adjust how much rub you use accordingly.

Herb Blend or Rub

6 Tbsp freshly chopped sage

1 Tbsp freshly chopped thyme

3 Tbsp freshly chopped sweet marjoram

2 Tbsp freshly chopped parsley

1. Combine together. This mix will keep up to one week in the refrigerator.

2. If there's still any left after one week, sprinkle over slightly moistened bread cubes to make a quick stuffing that can be easily frozen and warmed up later.

Sage Cream Cheese Spread

½ C fresh sage chopped

1 clove garlic minced

2 (8 oz.) packages cream cheese softened

3 Tbsp frozen lemonade concentrate, thawed – or lemon juice to taste

1. Combine the fresh sage and garlic.

2. Mix into cream cheese.

3. Add lemonade or lemon juice.

4. Refrigerate 24 hours before serving.

5. Tops crackers, breads, bagels, cucumber slices or use in canapés.

Shrimp Canapé Appetizers

1. Make up some cream cheese spread (recipe above)

2. Add peeled, deveined and chopped shrimp on top of the spread.

Shrimp Toast Appetizers

1. Make up some cream cheese spread (recipe above).

2. Spread the spread (with or without chopped shrimp) two slices of de-crusted bread.

3. Brown in oil (like a grilled cheese sandwich) for approximately 2 minutes.

4. Drain on paper towels and then cut into serving pieces.

Roast Goose or Turkey with Stuffed Mashed Potatoes

1 goose or turkey, ½ pound per person
½-1 potato per person
dried herbs
butter
string
salt
herb rub

1. Make mashed potatoes. (optional) Sprinkle a few teaspoons of the herb rub with a little dab of butter.

2. Wash the bird well, especially the inner cavity.

3. Dot the inside with butter, salt and herb rub. Stuff with the mashed potatoes.

4. Secure the skin back on tightly with a toothpick before roasting or thread a large eyed needle and sew it shut.

5. If cooking goose be sure to place on a dripping rack in the roasting pan. This will help the grease drain.

6. Bake at 350 degrees for 20 – 25 minutes per pound of fowl.

7. Baste often with juices while roasting to ensure that it does not dry out.

8. (optional) Secure either bacon or apple slices on the breast to prevent it from over roasting. These are removed the last 20 minutes of roasting.

9. Test with a meat thermometer to ensure that all of the bird is thoroughly cooked.

Wild Rice Stuffing

    3 C cooked wild rice

    1 medium onion chopped fine

    1 stalk celery chopped fine

    ¼ C melted butter

    ½ C chopped pecans

    1 C dried cranberries, apricots or cherries

    1 lb browned and drained pork or turkey sausage

    ½ tsp sage herb rub (or poultry seasoning)

    1 C chicken broth

1. Brown and drain the sausage and set in paper towels to absorb excess grease.

2. Sauté onion, celery and dried fruit in butter and add herb seasoning.

3. Dump the entire pan into the cooked wild rice and mix.

4. Wipe the excess grease off the sausage and add to this mixture.

5. Moisten by slowly adding ½ to 1 cup of the chicken broth to the mixture until it holds together.

6. Put dressing in a buttered 1½ quart casserole dish and bake covered 350 degrees for 30 minutes.

7. Uncover and bake an additional 10 minutes or until the top is browned.

Wedding Dinner – Chicken

Here is a less formal wedding dinner menu:

Wedding Feast Menu

Scallops wrapped in bacon (appetizer)
Herb brined chicken
Mashed potatoes with garlic & thyme

Scallops Wrapped in Bacon with Lemon Verbena

10 to 20 lemon verbena flower heads washed and patted dry.
1½ lbs fresh bay scallops
2 lemons
½ lb bacon

1. Slice lemon and remove rind.

2. Cut pulp in 3/8″ pieces.

3. Cut bacon in half.

4. Place a piece of lemon pulp on scallop.

5. Wrap both with a bacon strip and secure with a toothpick.

6. Broil for about 7 – 9 minutes until bacon is golden brown.

7. Slide one lemon verbena flower head on the toothpick to serve.

Herb Brined Chicken

> 1 whole cut up chicken
> 1 C kosher salt
> 1 onion halved
> 1 – 2 Tbsp garlic
> Pepper
> Fresh thyme

1. Mix salt and water until dissolved in a large bowl/ bucket. Some people heat this up and then let it cool before adding the poultry.

2. Add herbs, seasoning, and onion.

3. Mix well.

4. Add poultry.

5. Leave in fridge 12 - 24 hours.

6. Drain and bake uncovered at 400 degrees for 50 minutes or grill. Use a meat thermometer to ensure the poultry is cooked all the way through. Layer additional thyme over the poultry while it cooks.

Mashed Potatoes with Garlic & Thyme (serves 6-8)

> 12 potatoes peeled and quartered
> 1 small white onion minced
> 3 minced cloves of garlic
> 3 Tbsp butter
> ¼ C heavy cream at room temperature
> 1 Tbsp fresh thyme
> salt, pepper & butter to taste

1. Bring a large pot of water to a boil, add potatoes and boil until soft, about 20 minutes. Drain and set aside in a large bowl.

2. Sauté onion and garlic in butter until the onion is translucent, about 3 – 5 minutes.

3. Dump all of the frying pan ingredients into potatoes.

4. Add the rest of the ingredients and mix with an electric mixer or potato masher.

5. Season to taste with salt, pepper and butter.

Gift Opening Brunch

Some couples opt to open gifts at a separate party from the wedding and reception, often the next morning as part of a brunch. Palacsinta is like a crepe only a little heavier, but not as heavy as a pancake, and will work well with either a brunch or dinner menu. They work well for a crowd because they are economical, serve many and are good eaten cold or hot.

Brunch Menu

A variety of coffee and herbal tea

Scrambled eggs

Palacsinta with rosemary garnished with hawthorn flowers

Fresh fruit salad with mint for fillings or stand alone

Left over cake, breads, pies or rolls from the wedding dinner

Elderberry champagne

Rosemary Palacsinta (Hungarian Pancakes with Rosemary) (6-8 servings, about 18 pancakes)

2 C milk

4 large eggs

2 C all-purpose flour

½ tsp salt

1 tsp sugar

1 tsp dried rosemary (or cinnamon, poppy seeds, chives, thyme, basil or orange, lemon or lime zest)

1. Mix the flour, sugar, salt and rosemary. Beat the eggs and milk well.

2. Let batter sit for ½ hour.

3. Heat a small frying pan over medium-high heat. Spray the pan with cooking spray and let it warm about a minute.

4. Add a scant ¼ cup batter (I use three soup ladles) and swirl it around in the hot pan covering the bottom and filling in holes.

5. Cook about three minutes or until starting to brown around the edges, then flip it over and cook the second side until golden brown.

6. Butter each pancake and stack on a plate. They can be held at room temperature for several hours before filling them; do not refrigerate.

7. Palacsinta can be kept warm in the oven as you go – just lightly butter each one so that they don't stick together.

8. When ready to serve, fold into quarters, arrange at an angle on a plate, sprinkle with powdered sugar, drizzle chocolate syrup and accent with hawthorn flowers to serve.

9. Serve fillings in small dishes on the side. Here are some ideas:
    - fresh fruit compotes
    - canned fruit pie fillings warmed
    - jam or jelly
    - cooked chicken or seafood
    - scrambled eggs
    - rosemary with a chicken salad filling
    - raspberry fruit filling
    - chocolate sauce
    - whipping cream

These are fantastic in a buffet – stack the palacsintas high (maybe two varieties such as rosemary and cinnamon) and have a variety of fillings available with a fresh fruit salad. Let guests make their own concoctions.

Post Ceremony Sandwiches

Although the wedding couple often leaves for their Honeymoon shortly after the ceremony or the next morning, wedding attendees often stay an extra day or two to visit. Here are some post-wedding sandwich ideas (which can also be used to feed anyone that arrives ahead of the ceremony to help set up).

Lobster Roll

> One pound of lobster will make about four sandwiches.
>
> 1 pound boiled or steamed lobster meat chopped
>
> ¼ cup mayonnaise
>
> ¼ cup minced celery
>
> ¼ cup minced onion
>
> 1 Tbsp minced garlic
>
> Salt and pepper

1. Mix ingredients together.

2. Season to taste with salt and pepper.

3. Serve on hot dog buns, along with side plates of various garnishes, such as sprouts, tomatoes, thinly sliced cucumbers, dill pickles sliced the long way, and various slices of cheeses so that guests can top their own sandwiches.

Bread Machine Dinner Rolls (a dozen rolls)

½ C water
1 Tbsp water
1tsp water
3 large eggs
¼ cup butter or margarine, cut up
1 tsp salt
3-½ C bread flour or all purpose
3 Tbsp sugar
2 Tsp yeast
1 large egg, lightly beaten
1 Tbsp sugar

1. Add water, 3 eggs, butter, salt, flour, 2 Tbsp sugar and yeast to the bread machine in the order suggested by the bread machine manufacturer.

2. Select dough/manual cycle. When cycle is complete, remove dough from machine to a lightly floured surface.

3. If necessary add a little flour to make dough easy to handle and shape into round dinner rolls the size of a small orange. Place on a cookie sheet – sprinkle a towel with a little flour and cover the rolls.

4. Set on top of the oven while it is preheating or another warm place and let the rolls rise until doubled in size. This should take about 30 minutes.

5. Combine lightly beaten egg with sugar and brush onto the tops before baking at 375 degrees for 12 – 14 minutes.

Crock Pot Hot Turkey Breast Sandwiches

Purchase turkey breast counting on about one quarter
pound per person. This recipe is for a 3 -4 pound skin-
on-breast turkey roast and will serve 12 -16 people.

Skin-on turkey breast

1-2 Tbsp olive oil

4 sprigs fresh thyme or 2 Tbsp dried thyme

4 sprigs fresh sage or 2 Tbsp dried sage

2 cloves garlic minced or 1 tsp powdered garlic

1 small onion chopped fine or 1 Tbsp onion powder

1 stick butter – cold – with half of the stick cut into ½"-
thick squares

Salt and pepper

(optional) Monterey Jack cheese

(optional) cranberry sauce

1. Wash and pat dry turkey breast.

2. If using dried herbs, onion and garlic, mix together
into a rub with the salt. Rub the turkey breast with
the mixture. For added flavor, lift the skin where possible and add the rub. Slide a pad of butter between
the meat and skin and also in crevices.

3. If using fresh herbs and garlic, place some into the
turkey and some on the bottom of the crock pot.

4. Add turkey breast, skin side up, in the crock pot.

5. Drizzle with olive oil and the remaining fresh herbs.

6. Butter and turn slightly every hour.

7. Cook on high 2 hours and then turn to low another
2 hours.

8. When juices run clear, remove from the turkey from the crock pot and let cool in the refrigerator. DO NOT COOL AT ROOM TEMPERATURE.

9. Clean out herbs and any bones, skin, etc., from the crock pot, leaving the juice.

10. Shred turkey breast with a fork, and add back to pot in 2" layers, dotting with butter and sprinkling each 2" layer with salt and pepper.

11. Heat the mixture.

12. Serve hot on bread machine dinner rolls with cranberry sauce and thin slices of Monterey Jack cheese.

Crock Pot Pork Sandwiches

Purchase pork roast counting on about one quarter pound per person. This recipe is for a 3 -4 pound roast and will serve 12 -16 people.

1-2 Tbsp coconut oil for braising roast

1 pork roast

1 Tbsp orange zest

1 tsp coriander

2 Tbsp honey

½ stick butter, softened

2 cloves garlic, diced

1 white onion, diced (Vidalia preferable because of the sweetness)

½ C brown sugar

1 tsp dry mustard

Salt and pepper

1. Make orange herbed butter by adding orange zest, coriander, and honey to softened butter and set aside.

2. Braise pork roast on all sides in coconut oil.

3. Remove the roast and add to crock pot.

4. Sauté onion and garlic in pan used to braise roast until just softened.

5. Sprinkle brown sugar and mustard in pan along with one half of the orange herbed butter, stirring well.

6. Simmer until brown sugar is melted and pour over pork roast in crock pot.

7. Cook on high 2 hours and then turn to low 4 - 6 hours.

8. Spread orange herbed butter to the top and stir occasionally during last 4 – 6 hours or until falling apart easily with a fork.

9. Cool enough to allow you to shred the roast apart with a fork.

10. Put back into crock pot to keep warm.

11. Serve with Mango Salsa (recipe follows) on bread maker dinner rolls or ciabatta roll.

Mango Salsa

    1 lime
    1 – 2 ripe mango's peeled, seeded and chopped
    ¼ C chopped and seeded red pepper
    ¼ C chopped red onion
    1 medium sized jalapeno pepper seeded and chopped
    fresh cilantro, chopped

1. Mix all together except fresh cilantro.

2. Squeeze fresh lime juice over mixture (about 2 Tbsp)

3. Chill for 24 hours before serving to allow the flavors to blend.

4. Serve with fresh chopped cilantro on the side for guests to add as desired.

This salsa is great with pork chops, chips, veggies or as a sandwich topper.

Avia Lukacs & Therese Francis

Appendix A
Culinary Herbs

Herb	Use With	Useful Information
Angelica	Cookies, cakes, muffins, jams, candies, salads and soups	Adding to rhubarb dishes will reduce acidity. Tastes somewhat like celery. Used in Iceland, Norwegian and Scandinavian cooking.
Basil	Eggs, tomatoes, pasta, chicken, fish and shellfish	Use leaves only. Used in Italian cooking. Flavors oils.
Bay Leaves	Meats, fish, potatoes, soups and stews	Use leaves only. Most well known used *bouquet garni*. Remove before serving. Flavors oils.
Borage	Salads and teas	Flowers can be eaten and used to decorate cakes. Tastes like cucumbers.
Caraway	Breads, cookies, cakes cheeses and stews	Has a nutty flavor. Seeds are used only.
Cardamom	Stews, soups, pastries, breads and pickles.	Strong flavor. Used in Scandanavian and Middle Eastern cooking. Seeds chewed to freshen breath and aid digestion.
Catnip	Salads and tea	Rich in vitamin C.
Chamomile	Tea	Flowers used for tea.
Chervil	Egg and cheese dishes, vegetables, soups, stews, fish, chicken and salads.	Used in French cooking. Looks a lot like parsley.

Herb	Use With	Useful Information
Chickweed	Salads, soups, stews and as a vegetable.	Tastes like spinach. High source of iron.
Chives	Cheese dishes, eggs, fish, vegetables, and salads	Mild onion like flavor. A garlic chive variety is also available.
Cilantro (Coriander)	Salads, salsa, fish, beans, chicken and vegetables.	Used in Middle Eastern, Indian, Oriental, Spanish and Caribbean cooking.
Cowslip	Salads, tea, wine, decorate cakes and as a garnish.	Use petals only. Used to decorate cakes.
Dill	Fish, cucumbers, carrots, vegetables, egg, cheese, potatoes, sauces and salads.	Used in Swedish cooking and pickling. Flavors vinegars.
Elderflowers or berries	Used in jams, jellies, wines, and salads or with fruit	The berries are a lot like grapes. The flowers are edible and used as a garnish and to decorate cakes.
Fennel	Pickles, pizza, spaghetti sauces, breads, cakes, lamb, fish and soups.	Sweet taste similar to anise.
Hawthorn	Berries in soups, chili's and eaten alone. Berries in fruit, jams, jellies, sauces, deserts. Flowers in salads, to decorate cakes and as a garnish.	Beans are much like lima beans in taste and texture.

Herb	Use With	Useful Information
Hop	Stews and Soups. Served as a vegetable with butter.	Used to flavor beer.
Horseradish	Fish, pork, beef, potatoes and sauces.	Root used to make horseradish sauce.
Hyssop	Salads, soups, sauces and tea.	Strong minty taste. Good tasting iced tea.
Lavender	Fruits, pastries, cookies and cakes.	Lavender sugar is used as decoration for deserts.
Lemongrass	Tea, fish, chicken and duck.	Used in Asian dishes.
Lemon verbena	Tea, cakes, cookies, muffins, and fruit salads.	Used to flavor oils and vinegars.
Lovage	Salads, stews, soups, poultry, beef, lamb and pork.	Can be eaten cooked as a vegetable and buttered. Tastes like celery.
Marjoram	Eggs, lamb, beans, sausages, stuffing, seafood, poultry, breads, soups, stews and sauces.	Sweet minty flavor. Used in French, Chinese and Asian cooking.
Mint	Fruits, desserts, jellies, candies, tea, punch, vegetables, salads, fruit and as garnish.	Used in all types of cooking. Can aid digestion and freshen breath.
Mugwort	Flowers used with eggs, fruits, duck, goose, pork and in beverages.	Used to flavor beer before hops. Spicy taste.

Herb	Use With	Useful Information
Nasturtium	Salads, cakes, sauces and as a garnish.	Used to flavor vinegars, slight pepper taste. Used in French cooking.
Oregano	Tomato dishes, pizza, spaghetti sauce, mushrooms, peppers, eggplant, squash, fish, soups, chicken, beans, cheese, eggs, soups and sauces.	Used in Italian, Mexican, and Greek cooking.
Parsley	Soups, salads, sauces, beef, pork, lamb, fish, vegetables and as a garnish.	Mostly used as a garnish worldwide, freshens breath.
Rosemary	Fish, potatoes, sauces, soups, breads, beef, lamb, veal, chicken, and turkey.	Strong flavor – tastes like pine. It is the only herb that can be cooked for a length a time without losing its flavor.
Sage	Turkey, chicken, beef, pork, veal, cheese, stuffing, and soups.	Many varieties available. Used in Italian cooking.
Savory	Tea, vinegars, butters, chicken, turkey, lamb, beef, pork, pears, squash, beans, cheese, and egg dishes.	Flavor similar to thyme but stronger.
Sorrel	Soups, sauces, salads, and fish and seafood.	Used in French cooking. Taste is similar to spinach.

Herb	Use With	Useful Information
Tarragon	Chicken, fish, eggs, veal, lamb, beef, mushrooms, asparagus, soups, sauces and salads.	Used in vinegars. Used in French cooking.
Thyme	Fish, chicken, turkey, beans, pork, beef, potatoes, stuffing, tomato dishes, soups, stews and vegetable dishes.	Very strong taste. Part of a *bouquet garni*.

Appendix B
Edible Flowers

Flower	Color	Taste
Alliums	Many colors and varieties	Onions
Angelica	White	Celery
Bee Balm	Pink or Red	Earl Grey Tea
Borage	Iridescent Blue and Pink	Cucumbers
Calendula	Gold Orange Yellow	Spicy
Carnation	White Pink Red	Spicy like nutmeg or clove
Chamomile	White petals with yellow centers	Light apple
Chevil	White flowers	Licorice
Chrysanthemums	Red White Yellow	Bitter greens
Clover	White with Purple Tinged Tops	Licorice flavor
Cornflower	Blue	Sweet to spicy
Dandelions	Yellow	Green, somewhat like spinach
Daylilies	Red Purple Yellow Orange	Sweet crunchy like zucchini
English Daisy	Purple	Green leaf
Fennel	Yellow	Licorice

Flower	Color	Taste
Fuchsia	Purple Pink White	Not much flavor
Gardenia	White	Sweet flower flavor
Gladiolus	Many Colors	Lettuce
Hawthorn Blossoms	Red White	Sweet
Hibiscus	Pink Yellow Red Purple	Tart like cranberry
Hollyhock	Many Colors	No flavor
Honeysuckle	Red	Berries are poisonous - DO NOT EAT
Impatiens	Many Colors	No flavor
Jasmine	Creamy Chite Color	Sweet
Johnny-Jump-Ups	White Purple	Sweet
Lavender	Purple	Lavender
Lemon Verbena	Cream Colored	Lemon
Flower	Color	Taste
Marigold	Orange Yellow Gold	Spicy
Mint	Purple	Mint
Nasturium	Red Yellow Orange	Spicy peppery

Flower	Color	Taste
Pansy	Many Colors with Face-like Markings	Mild sweet perfumy
Petunia	Many Colors	Flower
Primrose	Many Colors	Sweet
Rosemary	White	Pine
Rose	Red Pink White Peach Yellow	Rose
Safflower	Yellow with Orange	Saffron
Sage	Purple White Pink	Sage
Scented Geranium	Many Colors	Many varieties each with their own flavor
Snapdragon	Many Colors	Not much flavor
Squash Blossoms	Yellow	Sweet
Thyme	Pinkish Lavender	Lemon
Violet	Purple	Sweet

Contact Us

Share your thoughts, comments, and photos with us at weddingherbs@crossquarter.com.

About the Authors

Avia Lukacs

Avia Lukacs lives with her husband and mother in New Richmond, WI. She provides care for her mother, diagnosed with Alzheimer's in 2012, hangs with her granddaughters, and whenever possible escapes out to the garden. She is always creating new recipes or potions made from ingredients taken from the garden. When she can't manage an escape outdoors, she is indoors writing.

Therese Francis

Therese Francis is an herb educator. She has been using herbal medicines and products since being introduced to edible backyard plants while still in elementary school. This is her second book in the 20 Herbs Series. She lives in Santa Fe, NM.

www.ingramcontent.com/pod-product-compliance
Lightning Source LLC
Chambersburg PA
CBHW030016290326
41934CB00005B/368